RECORDED VERSIONS GUITAR

AUTHENTIC TRANSCRIPTIONS
WITH NOTES AND TABLATURE

**Transcribed by
LEN BRAUNLING
AND
JOFF JONES**

GEORGE BENSON

REVISED EDITION

Direction: Ken Fritz Management, Los Angeles/Ken Fritz & Pam Byers

COVER PHOTO: DEBBIE LEAVITT

ISBN 0-7935-2396-6

**HAL•LEONARD®
CORPORATION**

7777 W. BLUEMOUND RD. P.O. BOX 13819 MILWAUKEE, WI 53213

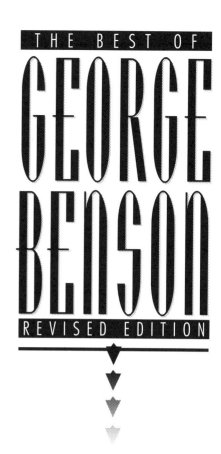

BIOGRAPHY

George Benson's crossover capabilities are a matter of record which has topped jazz, pop, and urban contemporary charts, often all at the same time. As close to a Renaissance man as modern music has ever produced, this pioneering guitarist and vocalist is equally adept at evading categories to create a musical genre wholly his own.

The tradition began in Pittsburgh, where George Benson began his musical career at age four by winning an amateur singing contest. At age eight, he was singing and playing ukulele on local street corners and, two years later, had landed a recording contract with RCA, for whom he cut several singles. At age 18, after hearing a recording by the legendary jazz sax player Charlie Parker, Benson developed an abiding love for jazz, landing a gig in Brother Jack McDuff's organ trio in 1963. Through his association with McDuff, he met a number of jazz greats, including John Coltrane and Kenny Burrell. It was guitarist Wes Montgomery, however, who served as Benson's greatest musical inspiration. Montgomery was to become the young musician's friend and mentor throughout the Sixties.

It was during the latter half of the decade and the first years of the Seventies that George's reputation as a uniquely talented guitarist grew. He recorded a number of albums for a variety of labels and graced LPs by such greats as Freddie Hubbard, Hubert Laws, Herbie Hancock, and Miles Davis. Much of Benson's best music from that period can be found on a series of six albums he recorded for CTI, including the Grammy-nominated *White Rabbit*.

Breezin' was Benson's first album on Warner Bros. records and it proved to be an auspicious debut. "This Masquerade," the only vocal on an otherwise instrumental album, became the first song in music history to hold the number one spots on the jazz, pop and soul charts. *Breezin'* went on to earn three Grammy awards in 1976, including Best Pop Instrumental and R&B Instrumental. It remains the best-selling jazz album of all time, having sold in excess of six million copies worldwide.

In Flight was George's million-selling, 1978 follow-up. Later that year, he scored another smash single with a live version of the Drifters classic, "On Broadway," from yet another platinum-selling album, *Weekend In L.A.*, featuring the original version of "The Greatest Love Of All." That album garnered him a Grammy for Best Male R&B Performance in 1978. *Livin' Inside Your Love*, Benson's 1979 offering, was followed a year later by *Give Me The Night*, which launched two more Top Ten hits, the title cut (number one on pop and soul charts) and "Love X Love." George's Grammy awards in 1980 included Best Male R&B Performance, Best R&B Performance, and Best Jazz Vocal Performance.

A compilation release, 1981's *The George Benson Collection*, yielded the number one single "Turn Your Love Around," followed by *In Your Eyes* in 1983, which features the Grammy award winning song "Being With You", and *20/20* in 1985.

Also in 1985, a compilation album of Benson's best love songs, appropriately entitled *Love Songs*, was released in the U.K. and immediately went triple platinum.

It was followed by *While The City Sleeps* in 1986, which prompted a command performance tour that attracted bigger and more enthusiastic crowds then ever before, as well as a pair of singles: "Kisses In The Moonlight" and "Shiver." Shortly after, Benson joined forces with fellow guitar great Earl Klugh for what was hailed as the jazz guitar line-up of the decade. The resulting album, *Collaboration,* went gold, while a subsequent tour of Japan and the U.S. packed houses at every stop.

Benson's tenth Warner Bros. Records release was 1988's *Twice The Love.* A reworking of Curtis Mayfield's classic "Let's Do It Again" as well as the title track, added two more notches to Benson's string of hit singles, while a follow-up tour of the U.S. and Europe established new box office records for the artist, including a historic series of six sold-out appearances at London's Wembley Arena.

It was while in England that Benson began working with legendary arranger Robert Farnon and members of the London Symphony Orchestra on a projected album of pop standards. While collaborating with Farnon, he also set to work on an album of jazz standards which quickly took precedence, thanks to the enthusiastic involvement of producer Tommy LiPuma as well as keyboardist McCoy Tyner. Benson thus turned his formidable talents to this collection of his favorite jazz material, resulting in the 1989 release, *Tenderly.* With additional arrangements by the renowned Marty Paich, this eight-song collection is a lovingly rendered tribute to Benson's own beginnings. The following European, Japanese, and U.S. tours with McCoy Tyner proved to be a critical rave.

The original album of pop standards was fused with an ongoing wish to recast some classic musical moments into a modern mold — that album is Benson's twelfth for Warners — *Big Boss Band*, featuring the legendary Count Basie Orchestra. Most recently Benson has released a new album, *Love Remembers*. A five vocal, seven instrumental collection, *Love Remembers* features performances by many jazz notables, including Freddie Washington, Phil Upchurch, and Randy Brecker. The album contains a song, "Come Into My World" that was cowritten by Benson and his son, Steven Benson Hue, while another son, Robbie C. Benson served as production assistant on the project. The album was produced, mixed, and engineered by such legends as Bob James, Bill Schnee, Al Schmitt, Elliot Scheiner, and Stewart Levine.

Basie's Bag

By George Benson

Before You Go

By George Benson

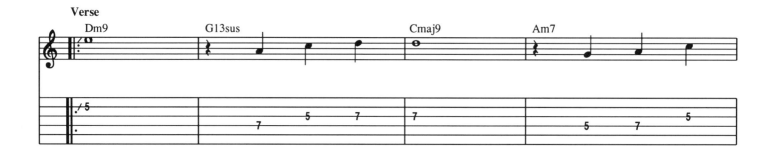

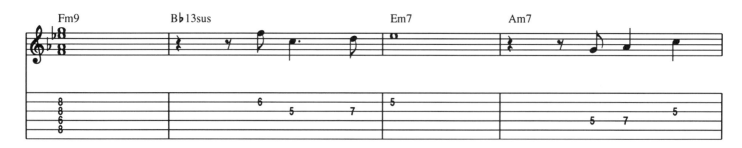

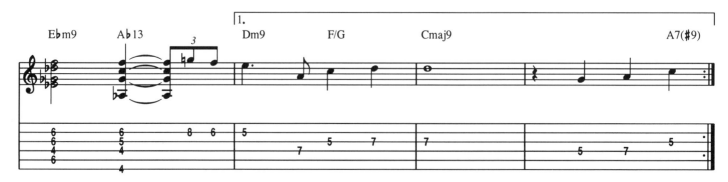

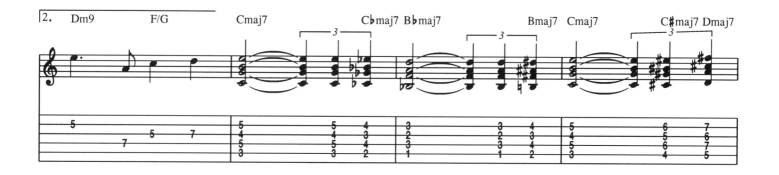

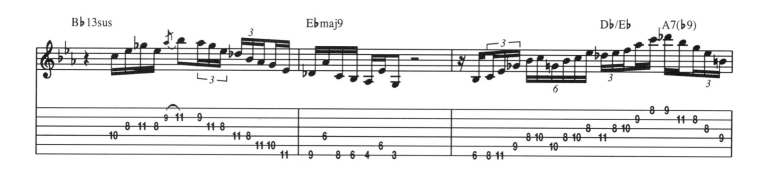

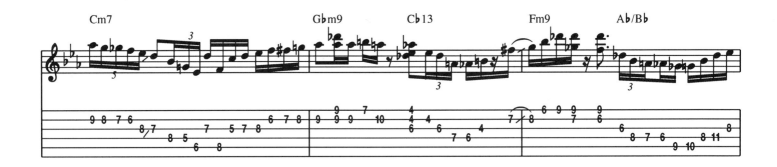

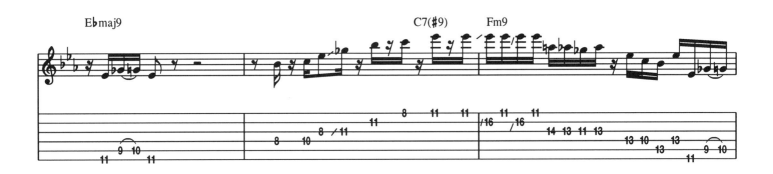

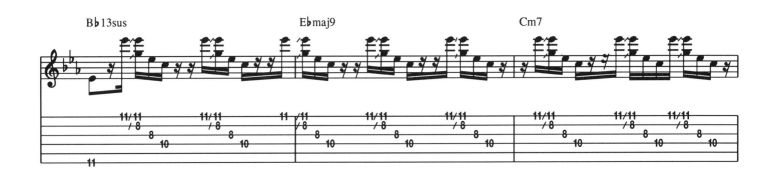

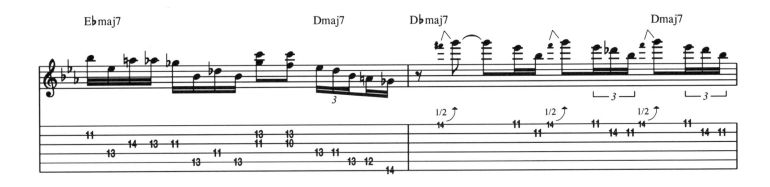

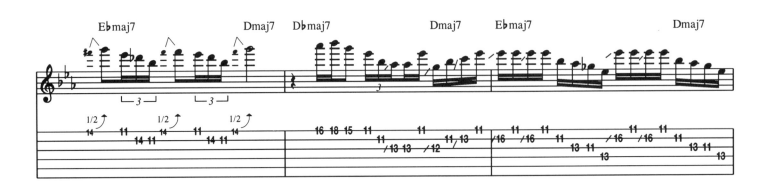

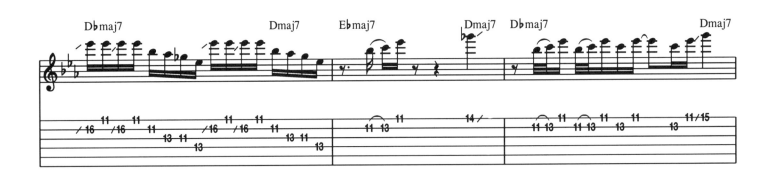

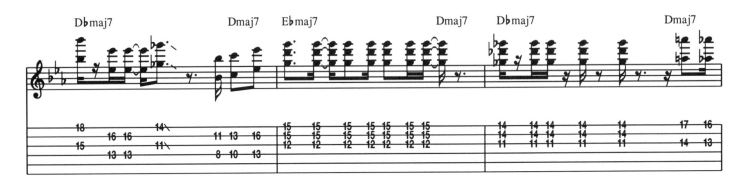

Beyond The Sea

English lyric by Jack Lawrence
Music and French lyric by Charles Trenet

D. S. al Coda

Coda

20

Breezin'

Words and Music by Bobby Womack

California PM

By George Benson

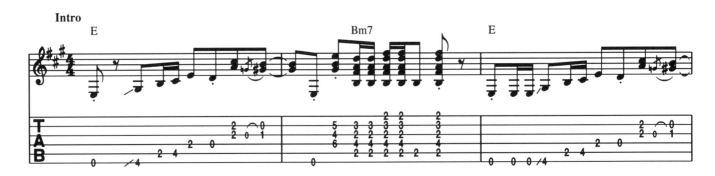

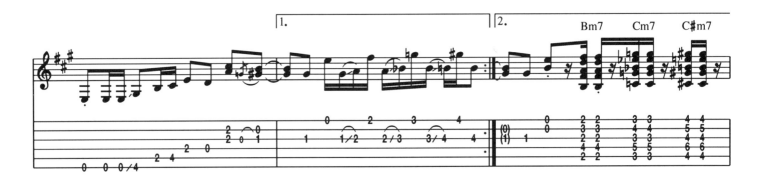

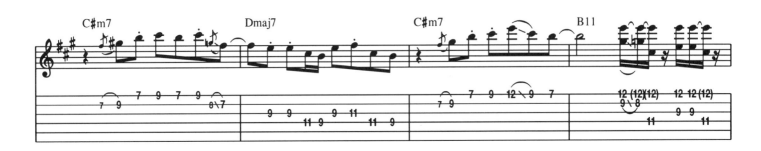

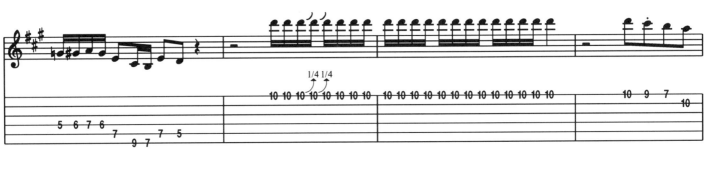

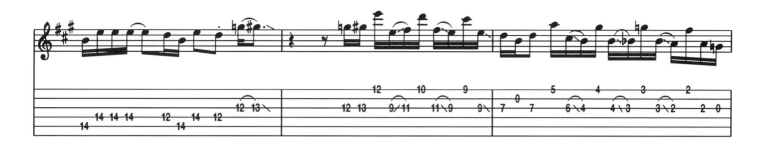

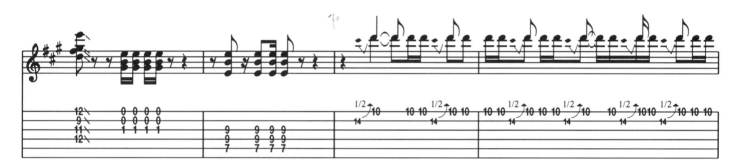

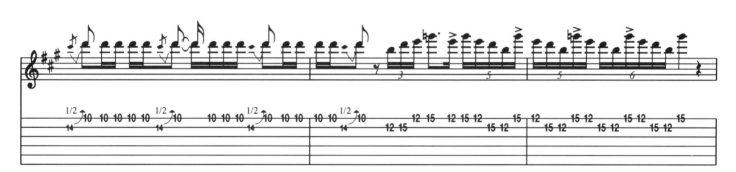

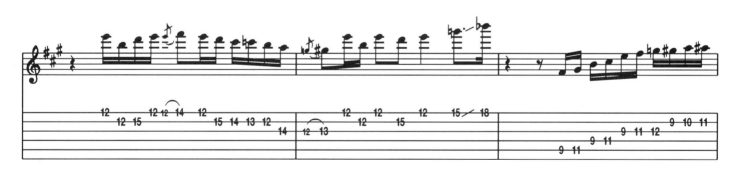

34

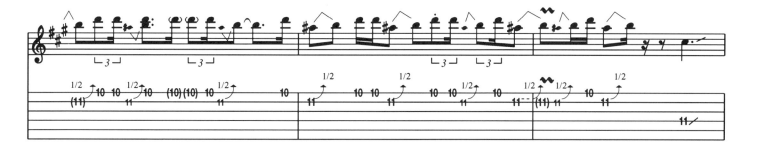

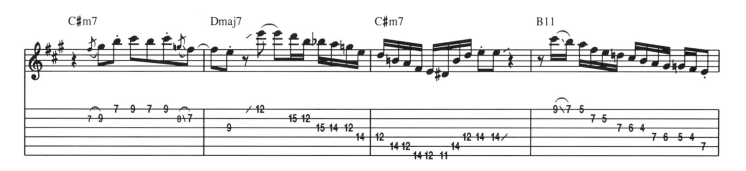
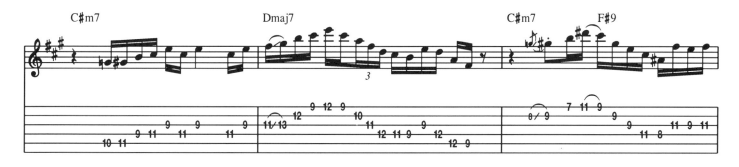

Feel Like Makin' Love

Words and Music by Eugene McDaniels

Chorus

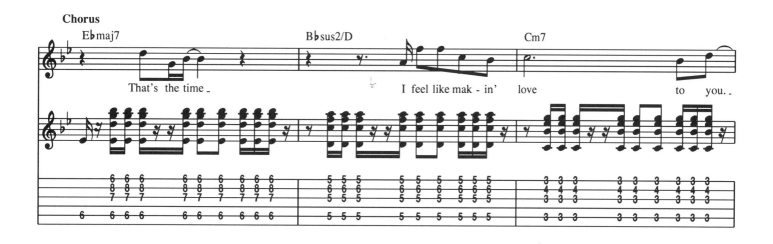

That's the time ___ I feel like mak - in' love to you. __

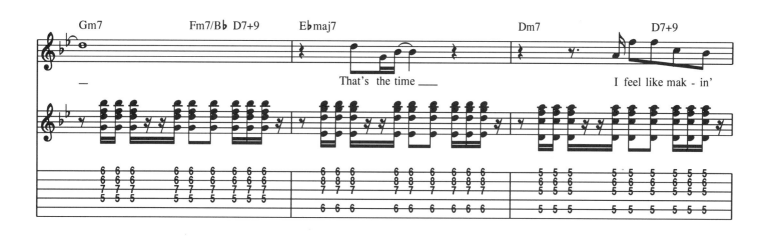

That's the time ___ I feel like mak - in'

dreams come true. __

Verse

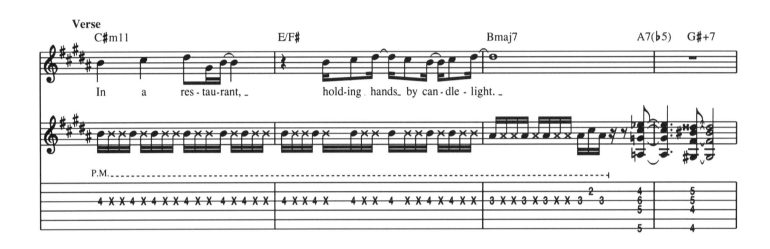

In a res-tau-rant, _ hold-ing hands _ by can-dle - light. _

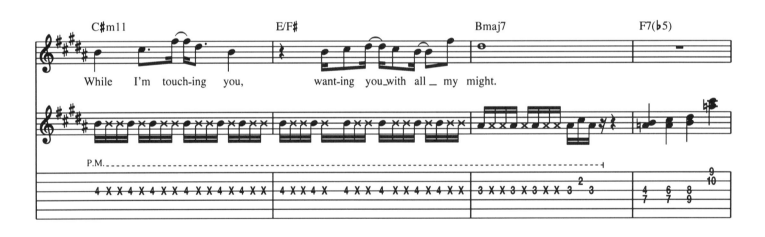

While I'm touch-ing you, want-ing you _ with all _ my might.

𝄋 Chorus

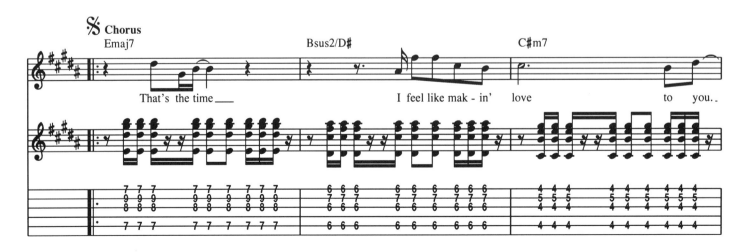

That's the time ___ I feel like mak - in' love to you.

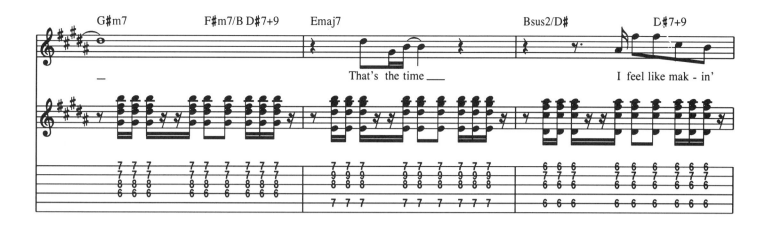

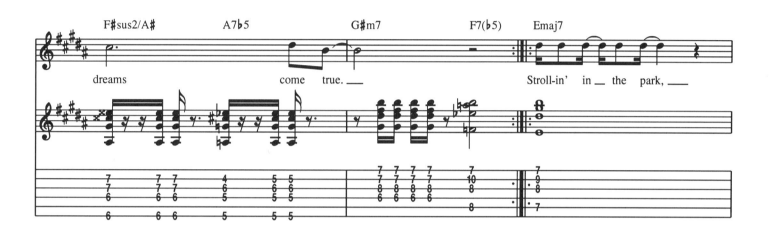

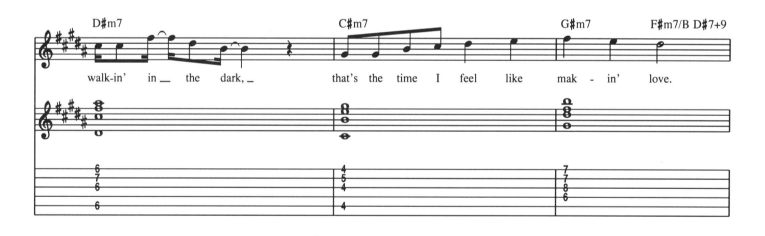

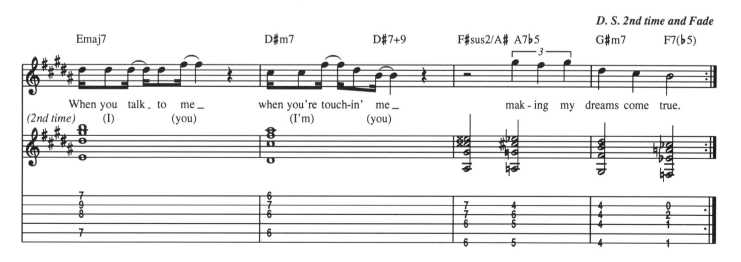

Give Me The Night

Words and Music by Rod Temperton

To Coda ⊕

Chorus

Guitar Solo

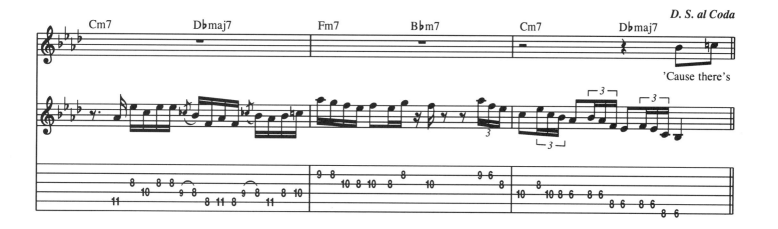

'Cause there's

⊕ *Coda*   **Verse**

— And if we stay to - geth - er,   we'll feel the

rhy - thm of the eve - ning tak - in' us up __ high. __ Nev - er mind the weath - er.

We'll be danc - in' in the street __ un - til the morn - ing __ light. __ 'Cause there's

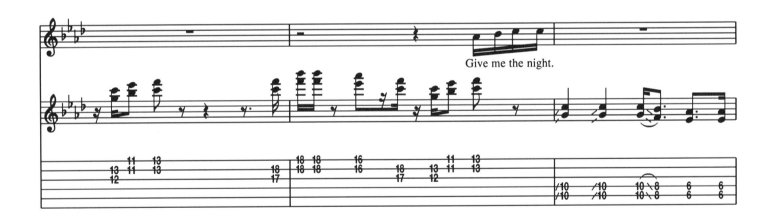

Here, There And Everywhere

Words and Music by John Lennon and Paul McCartney

MCA music publishing

Instrumental Verse

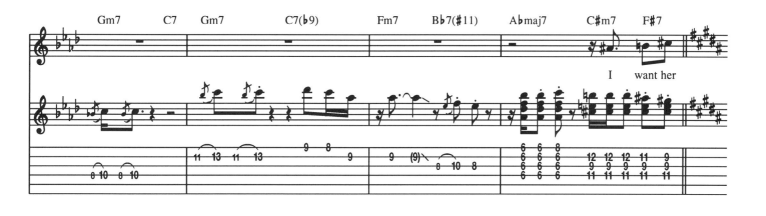

I want her

continue with funky rhythm playing

Bridge

ev-'ry - where,___ and if she's be-side_ me I know I need nev-er_ care. ___ But to love_ her is to meet her

Verse

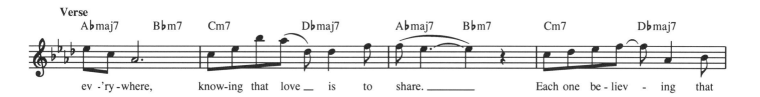

ev -'ry -where, know-ing that love __ is to share. _____ Each one be - liev - ing that

love nev-er dies, _ watch-ing her eyes ___ and hop-ing I'm al - ways there ___ to _ be _

___ there _____ and ev -'ry - where, _____ mm,. hmm. __

Here, there, _____ and eve-ry - where. _____ And eve - ry -

Free Time

where. _____

In Your Eyes

Words by Dan Hill
Music by Michael Masser

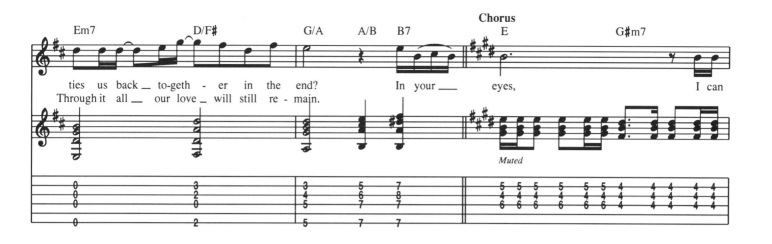

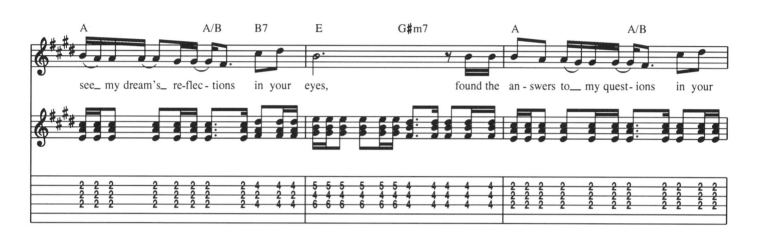

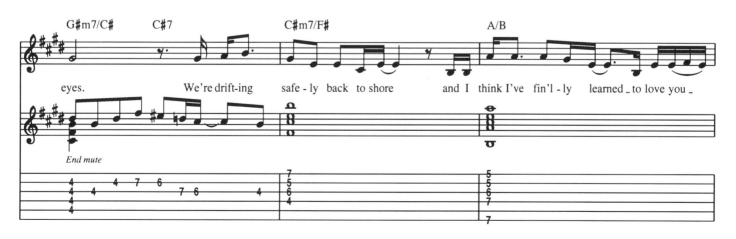

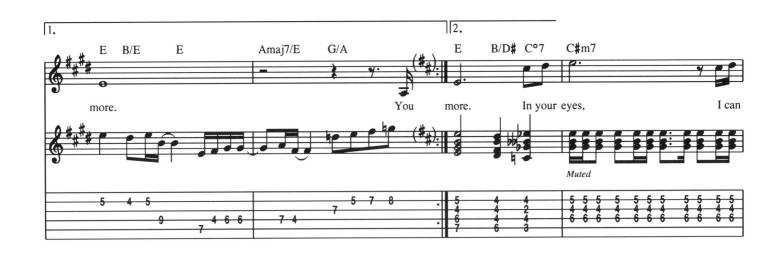

Lady

By Ronnie Foster

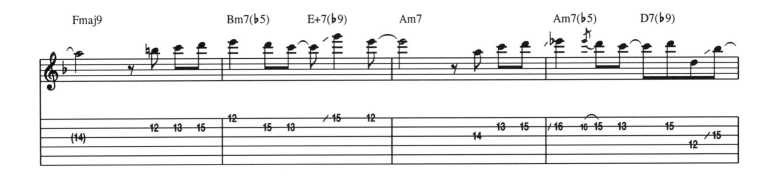

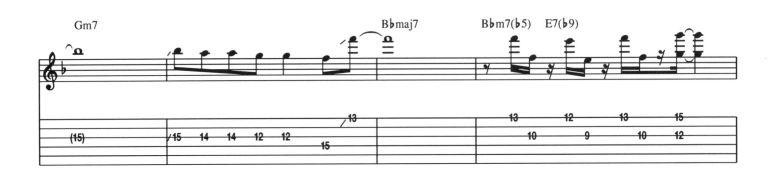

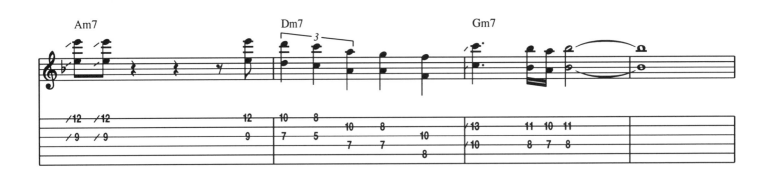

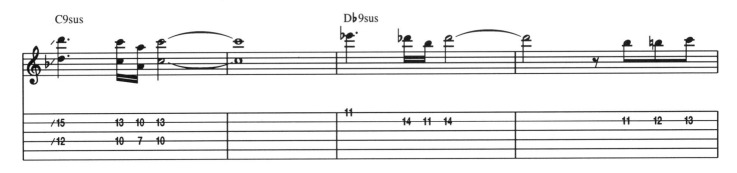

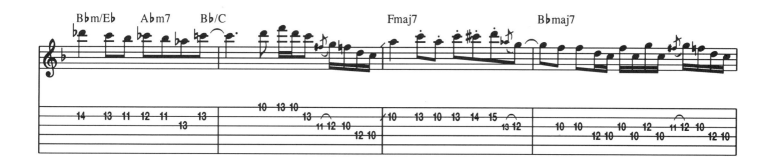

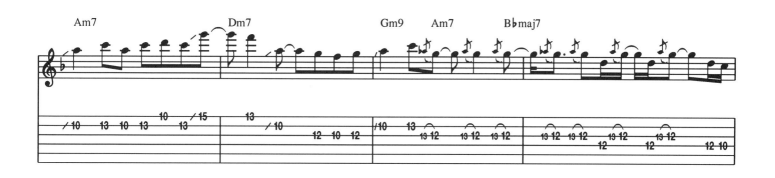

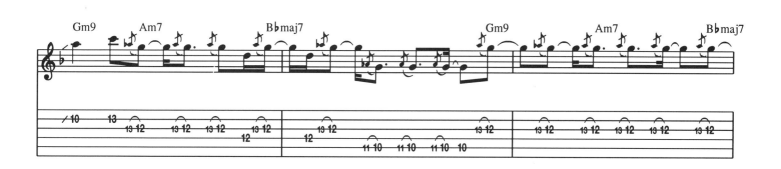

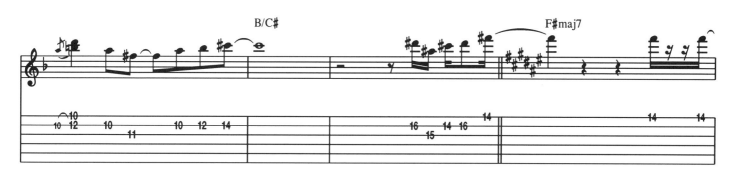

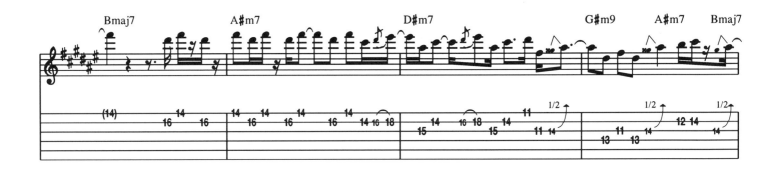

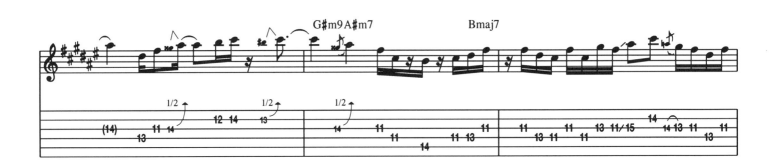

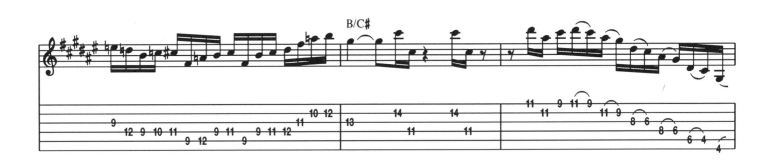

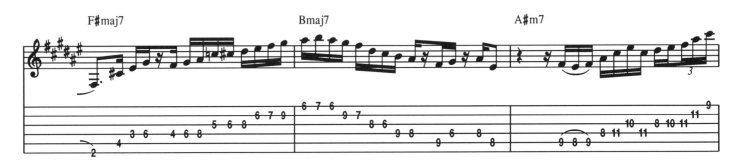

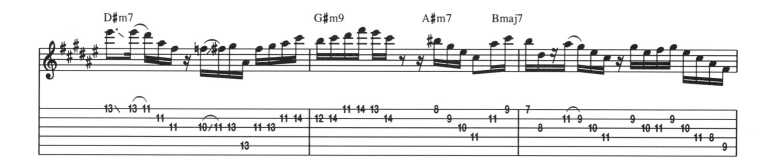

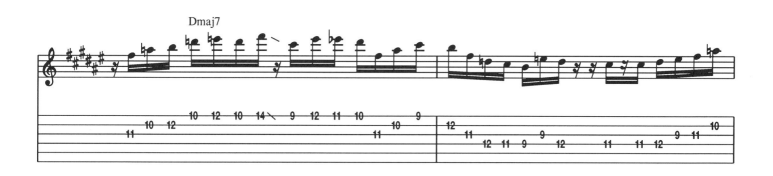

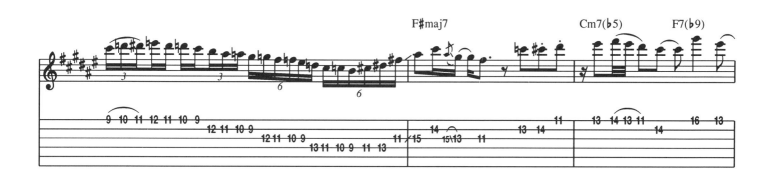

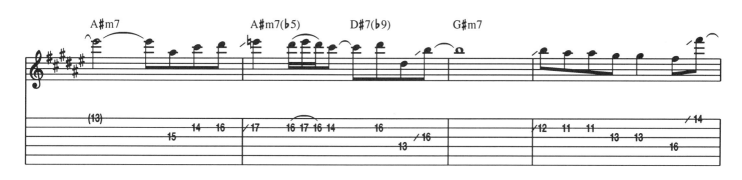

Lady Love Me
(One More Time)

Words and Music by James N. Howard and David Paich

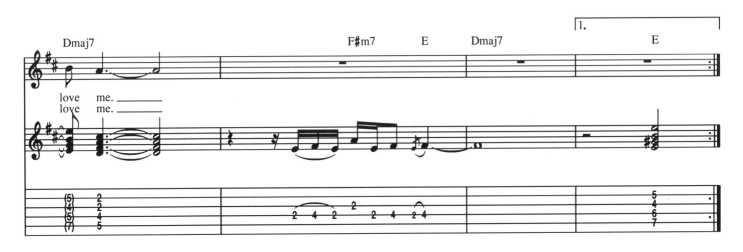

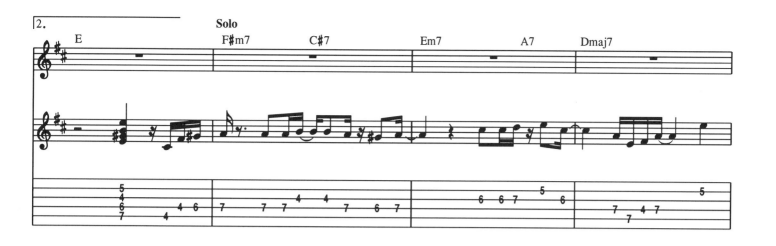

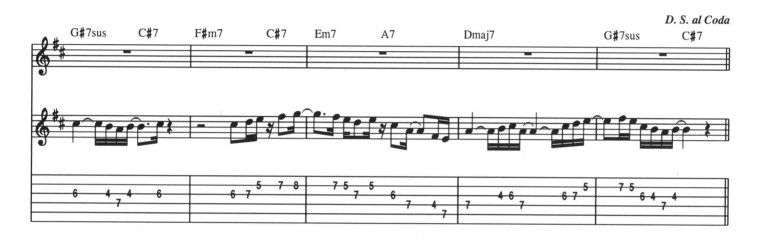

Coda

La — dy __ love me __ all the __ time. __ Love me, __ la — dy, __

all the __ time. __ Let me __ love you __ one more time. __

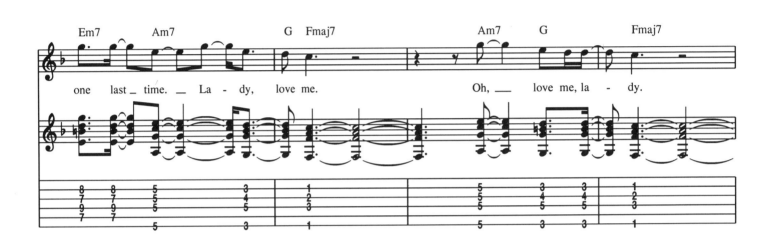

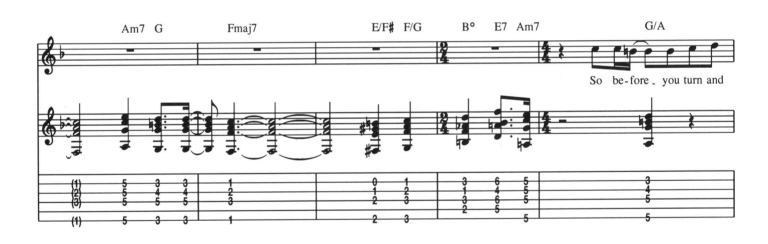

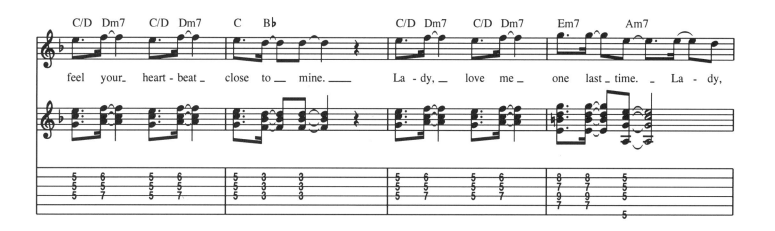

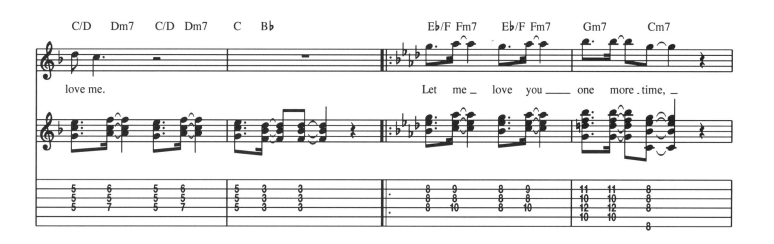

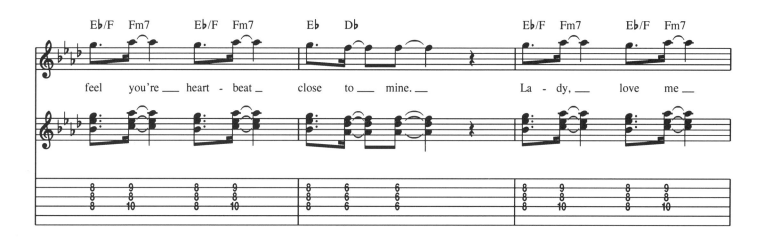

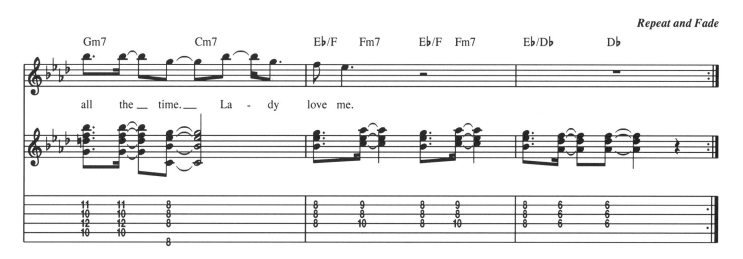

Love Ballad

Words and Music by Skip Scarborough

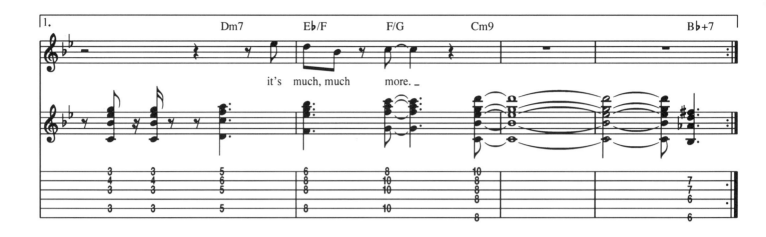

it's much, much more. _

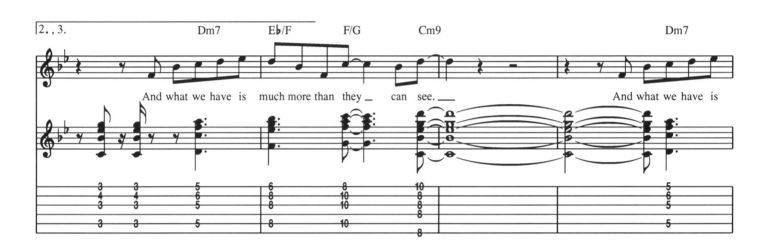

And what we have is much more than they __ can see. __ And what we have is

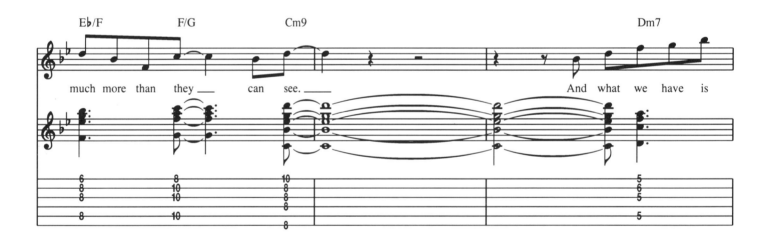

much more than they __ can see. __ And what we have is

To Coda ⊕

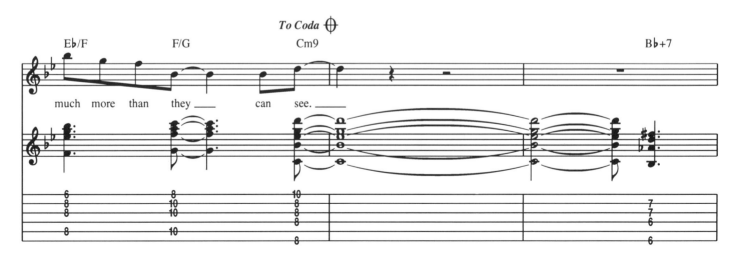

much more than they ____ can see. ____

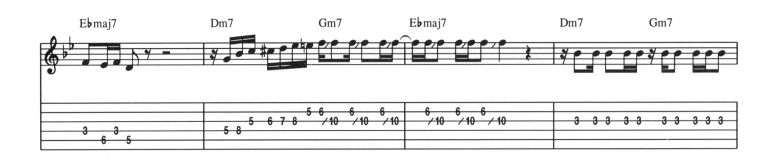

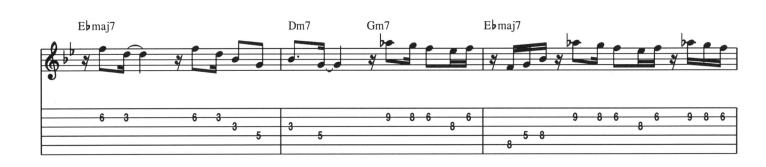

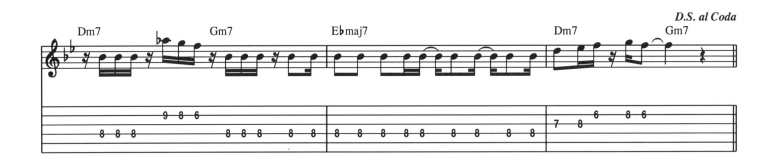

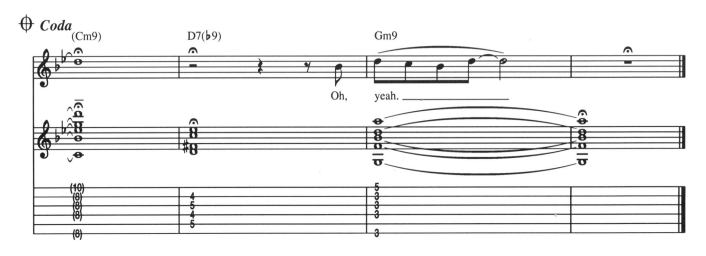

Mimosa

By George Benson

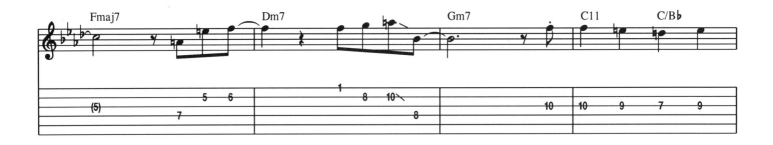

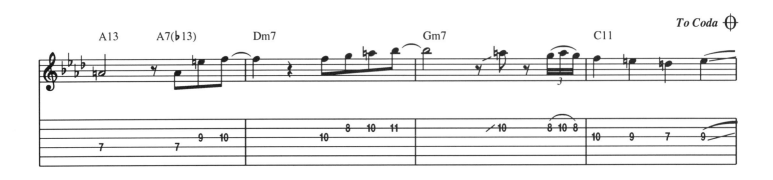

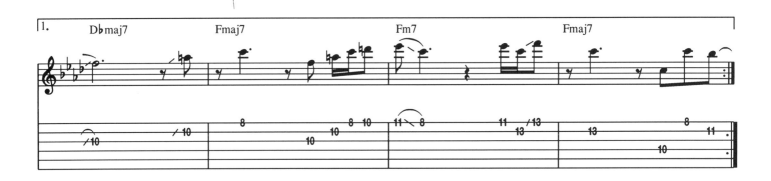

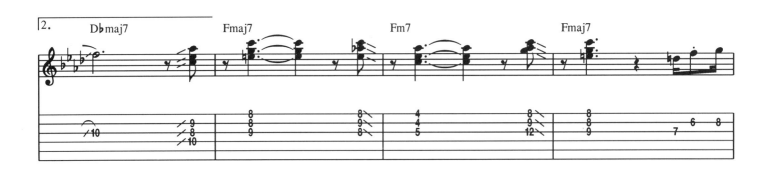

Photo: ROBERT HAKALSKI

On Broadway

Words and Music by
Barry Mann, Cynthia Weil, Mike Stoller, and Jerry Leiber

Lyrics:

They say the ne-on lights are bright on Broad-way;

they say there's al-ways mag-ic in ___ the air. ___

But when you're walk-in' down the street, ___ and you ain't had e-nough to eat, ___

the glit-ter rubs right off and you're_ no-where._

Interlude

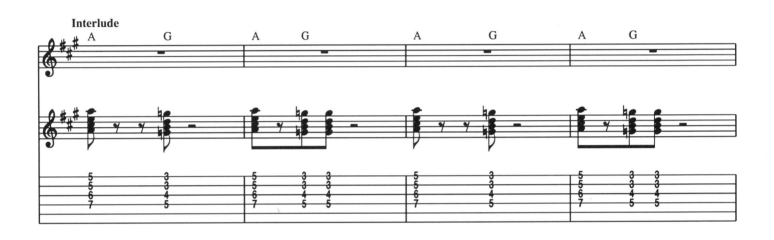

Verse

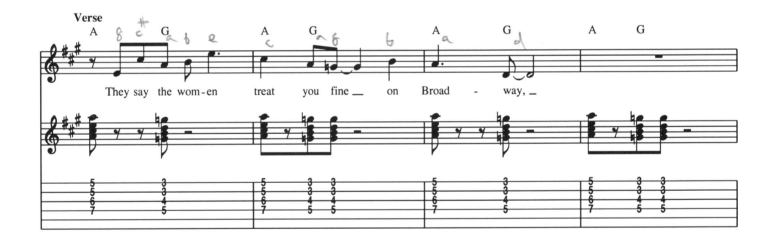

They say the wom-en treat you fine_ on Broad-way,_

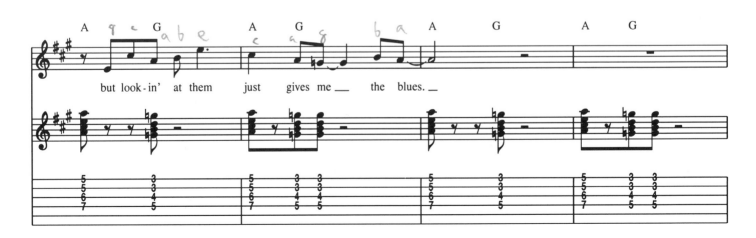

but look-in' at them just gives me_ the blues._

'Cause how you gon-na make some time _ when all you got is one thin dime, _

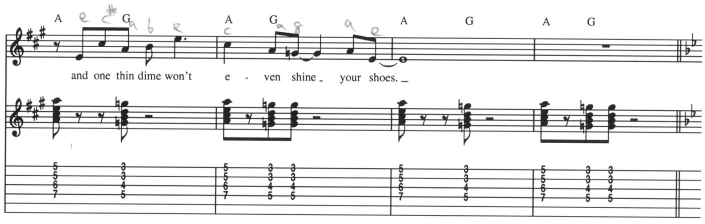

and one thin dime won't e - ven shine _ your shoes. _

Interlude

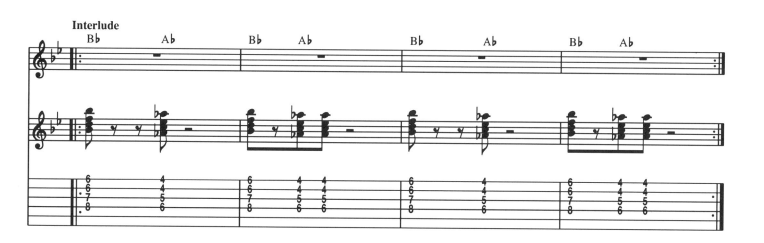

Verse

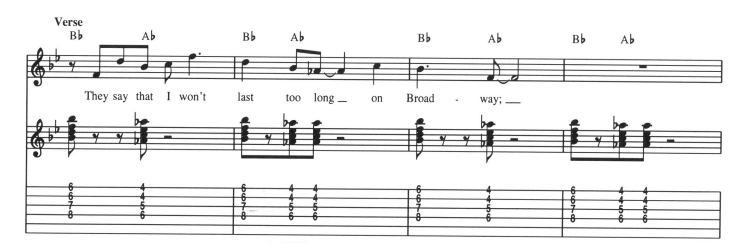

They say that I won't last too long _ on Broad - way; _

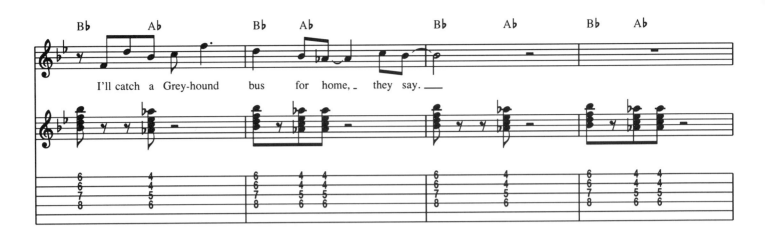

I'll catch a Grey-hound bus for home, they say.

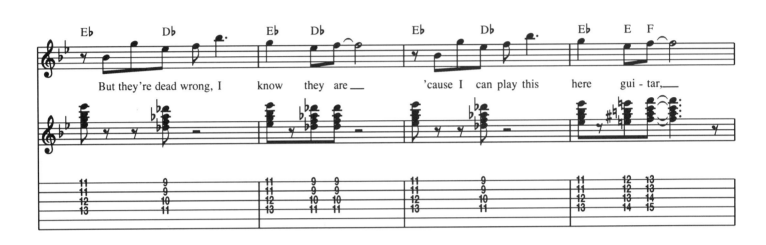

But they're dead wrong, I know they are 'cause I can play this here gui-tar,

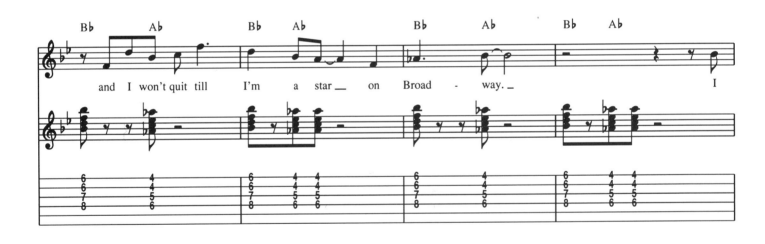

and I won't quit till I'm a star on Broad-way.

I

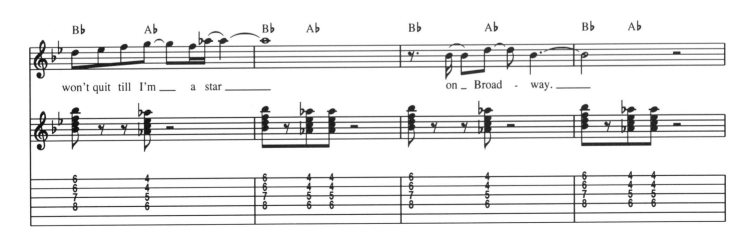

won't quit till I'm a star on Broad-way.

So This Is Love

By George Benson

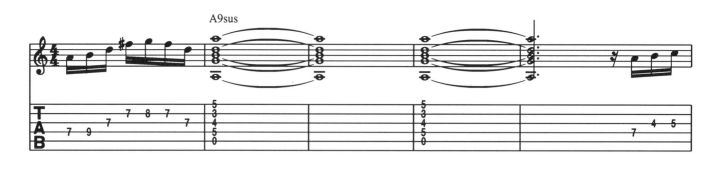

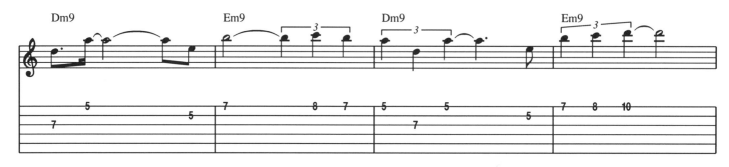

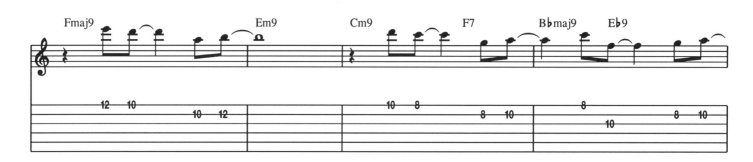

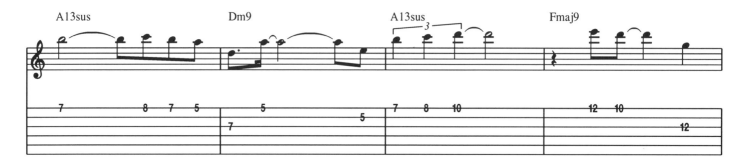

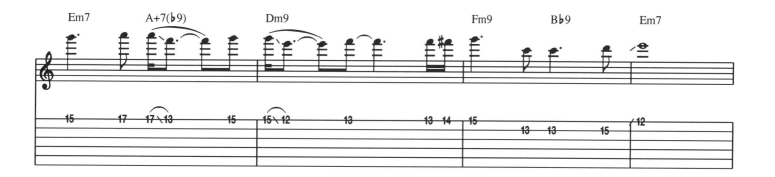

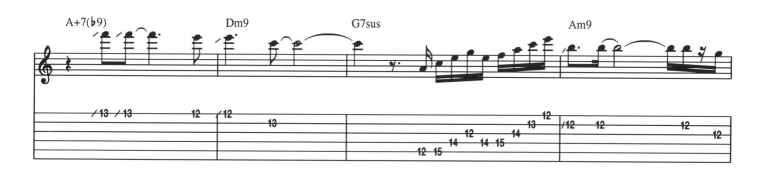

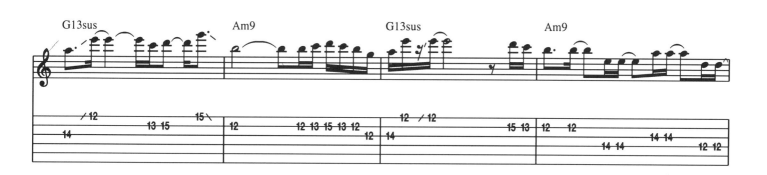

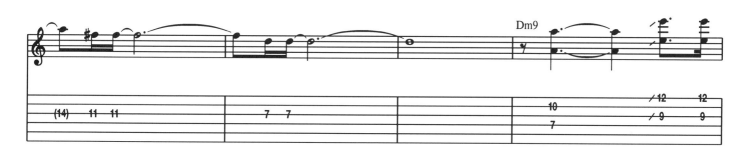

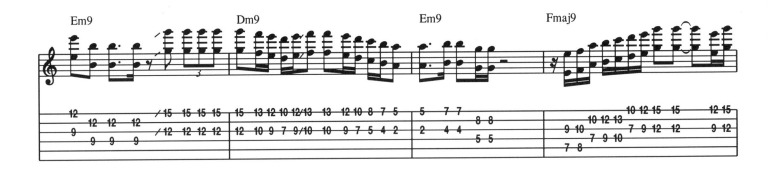

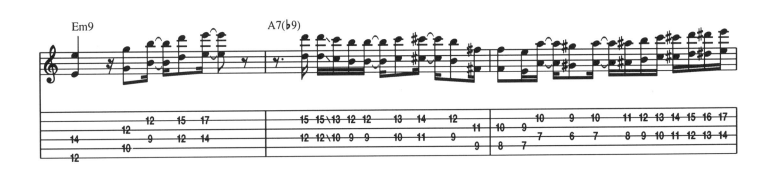

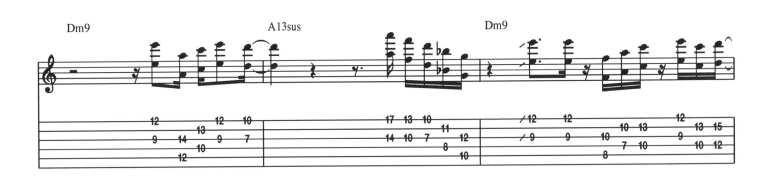

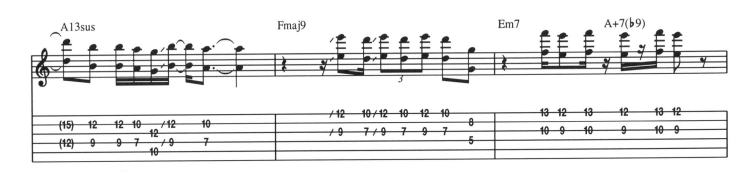

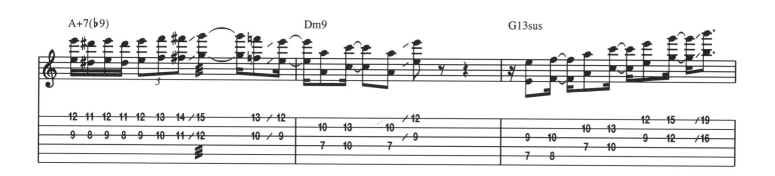
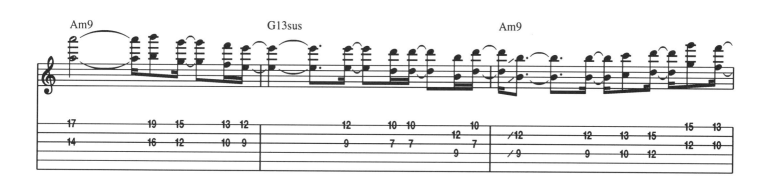

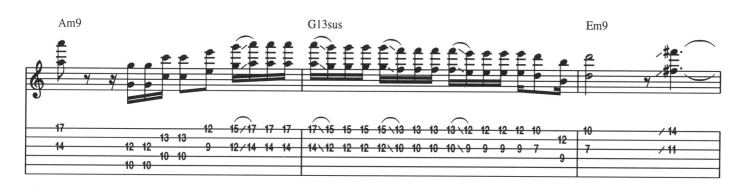

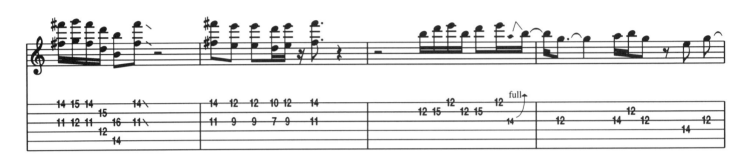

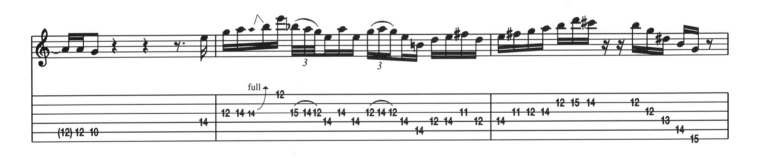

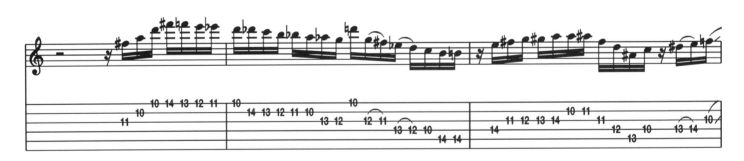

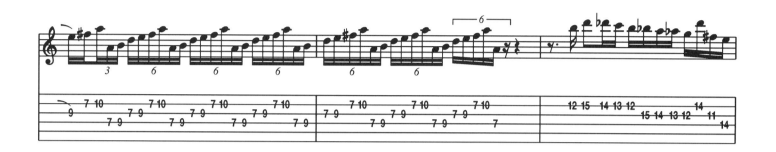

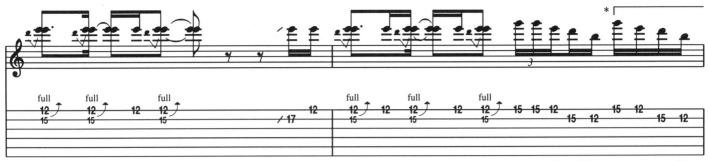

* play all 7 figures evenly across 5 beats

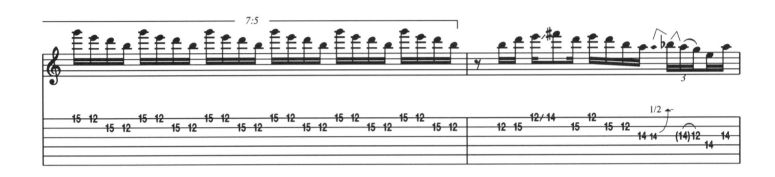

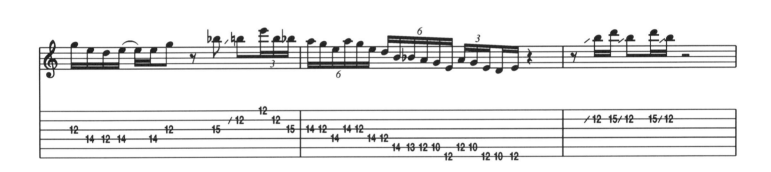

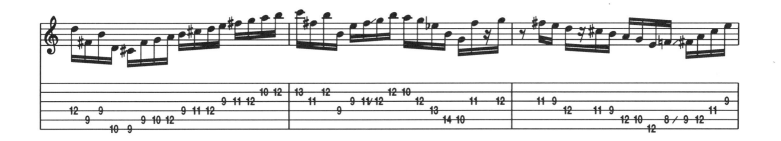

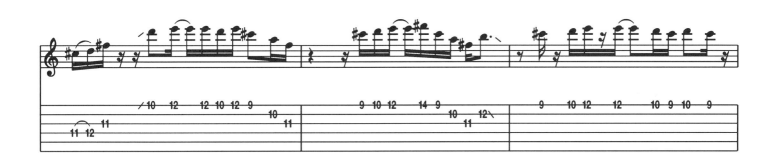

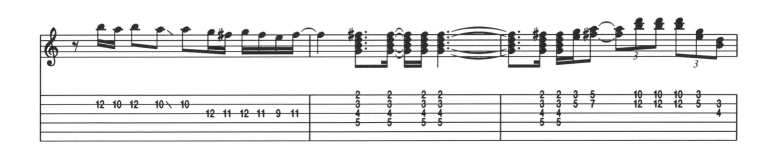

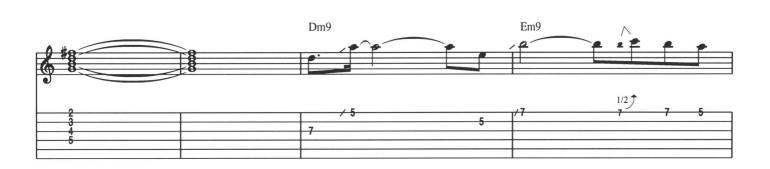

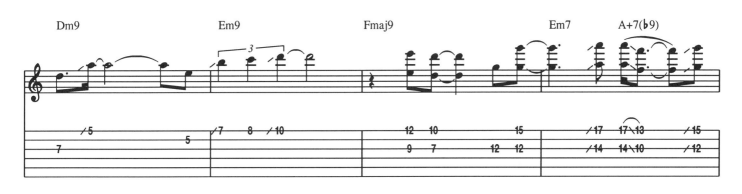

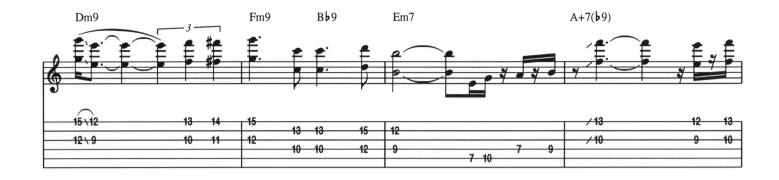

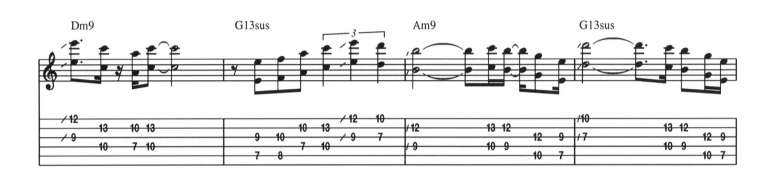

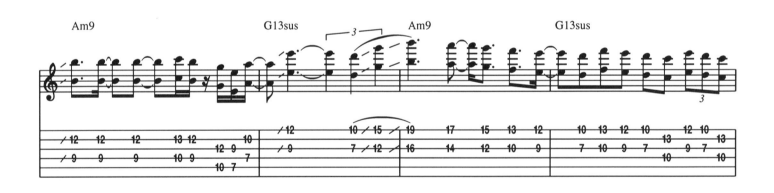

Repeat and Fade

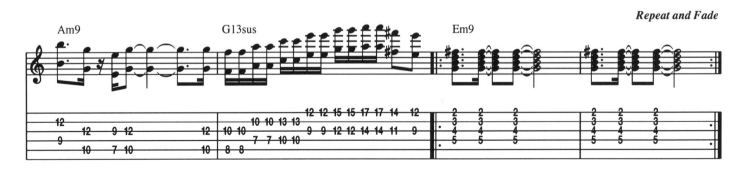

This Masquerade

Words and Music by Leon Russell

Are we real - ly hap - py here ___ with this lone - ly game we play, ___

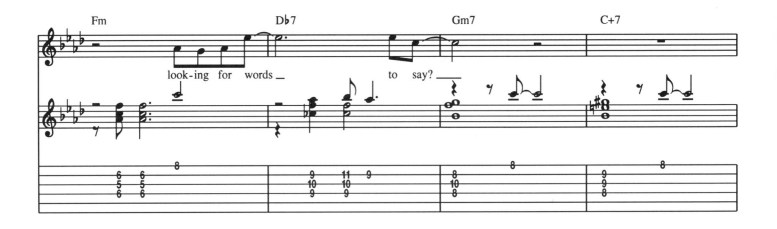

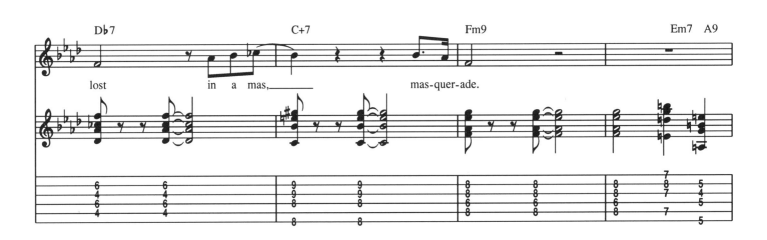

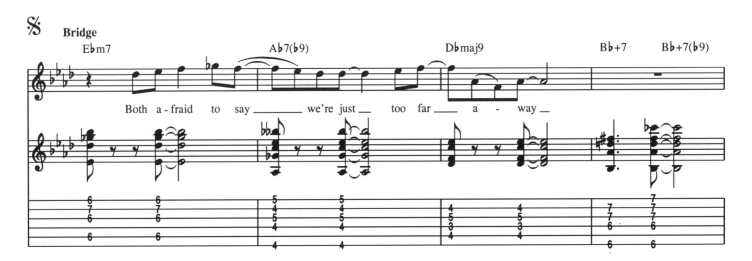

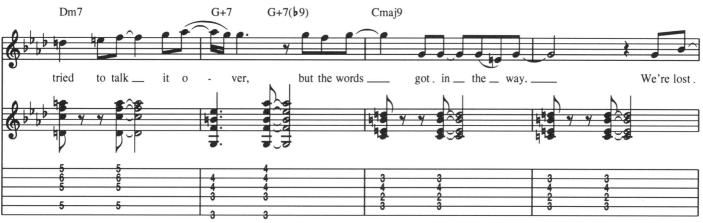

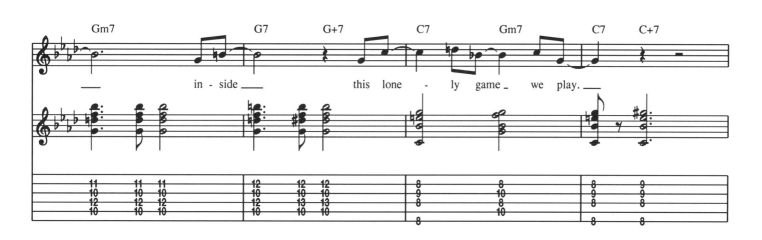

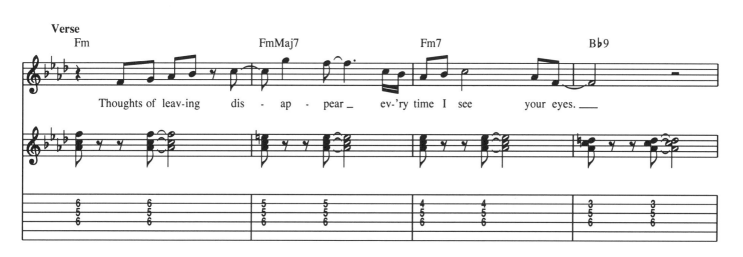

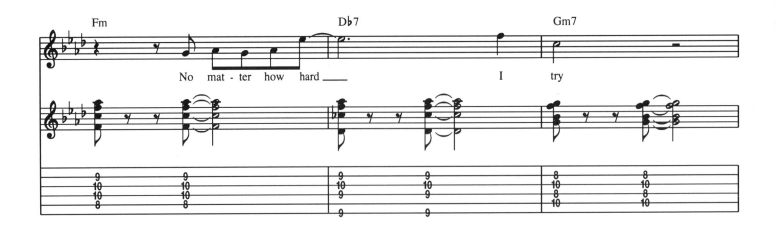

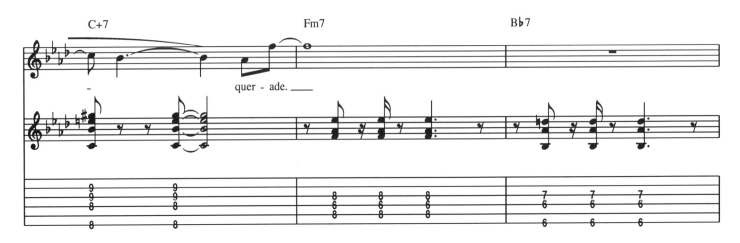

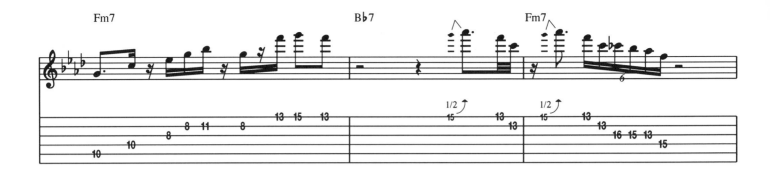

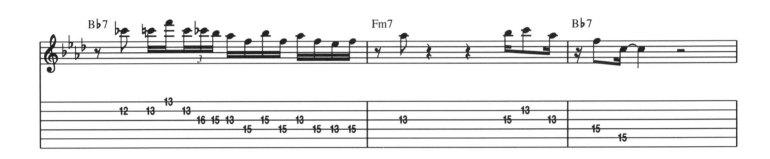

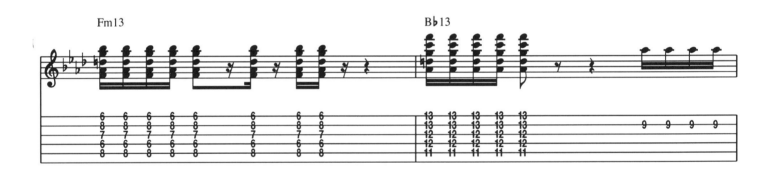

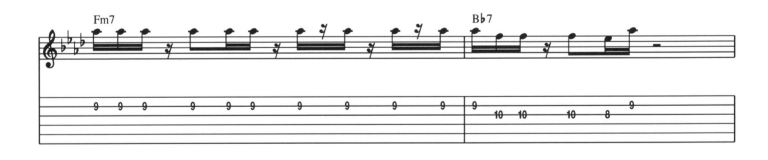

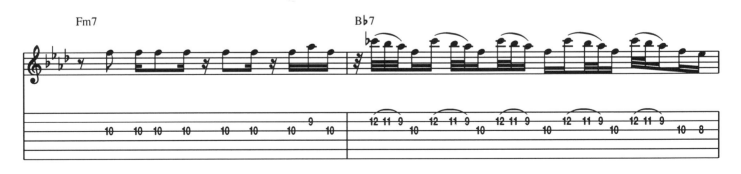

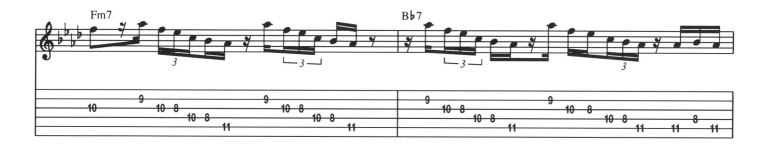

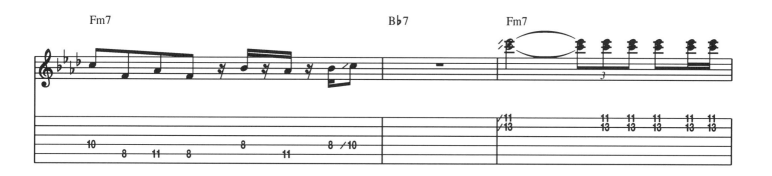

D. S. al Coda

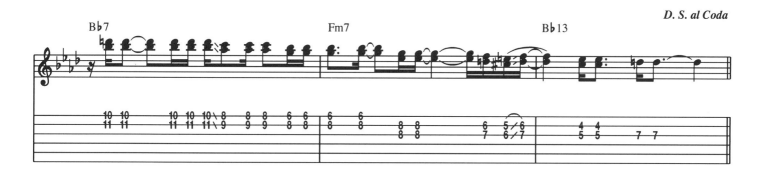

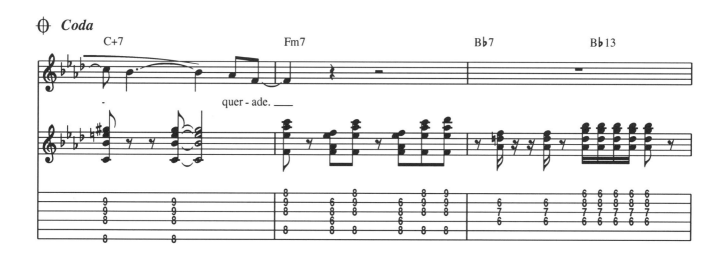

Repeat and Fade

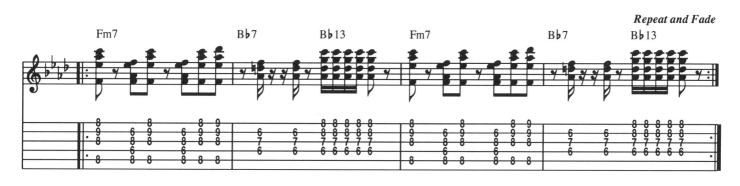

Turn Your Love Around

Words and Music by
Jay Graydon, Steve Lukather and Bill Champlin

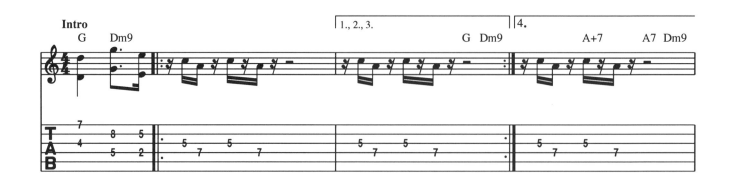

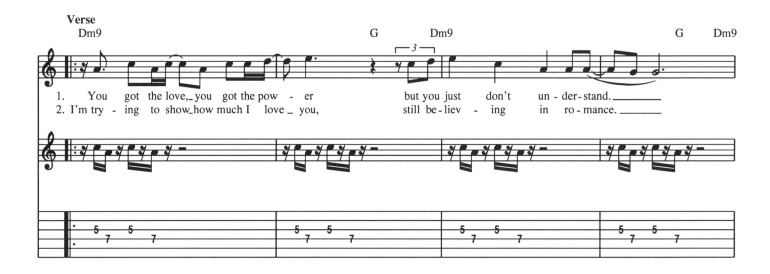

1. You got the love, you got the pow-er but you just don't un-der-stand.
2. I'm try-ing to show how much I love you, still be-liev-ing in ro-mance.

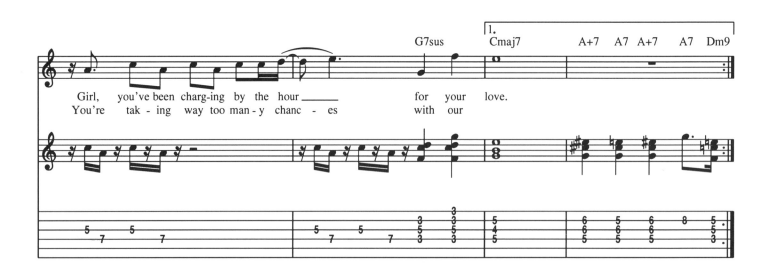

Girl, you've been charg-ing by the hour for your love.
You're tak-ing way too man-y chanc-es with our

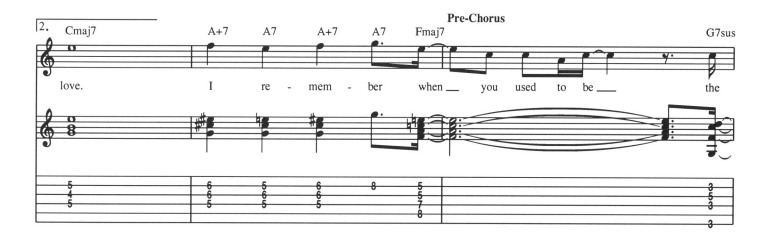

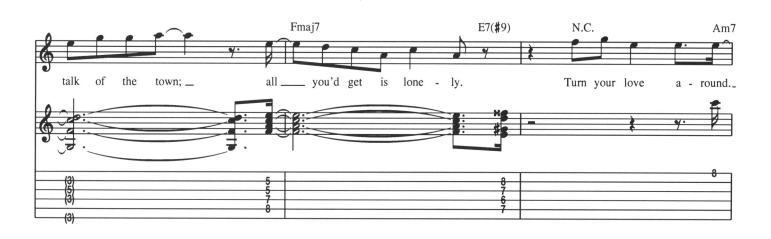

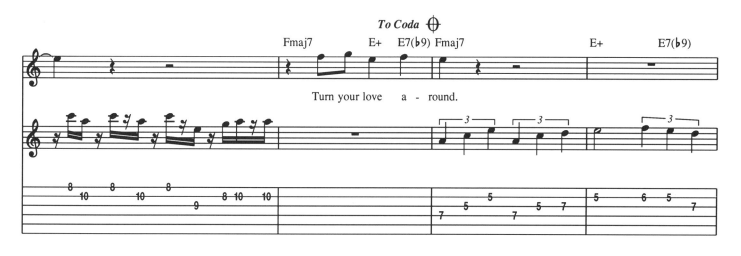

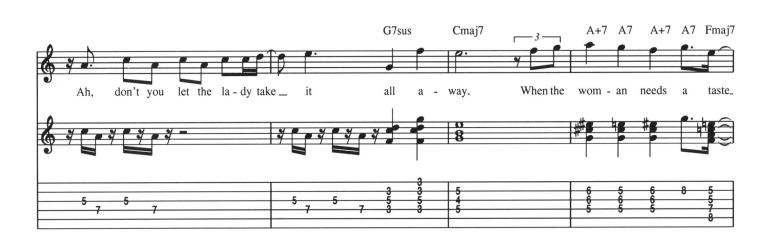

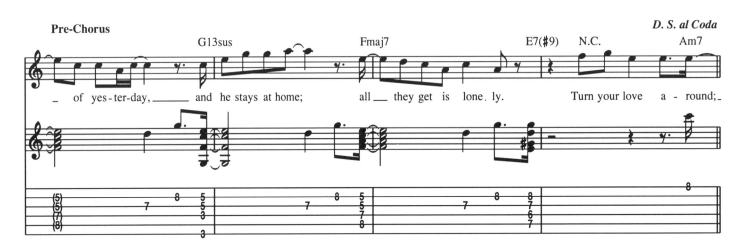

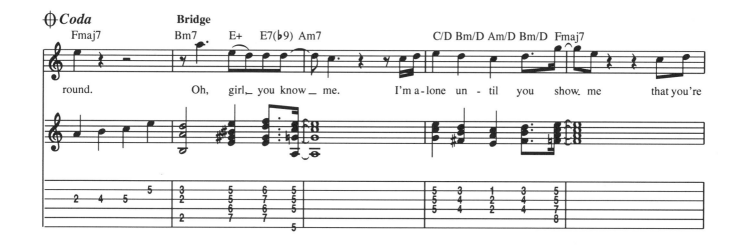

⊕ Coda   **Bridge**

round.   Oh, girl, you know me.   I'm a-lone un-til you show me   that you're

still in love with me.   We're gon-na make it,   we're gon-na take it back where we be-long.

Chorus

Turn your love a-round.   Don't you turn me down,   I can show you how.

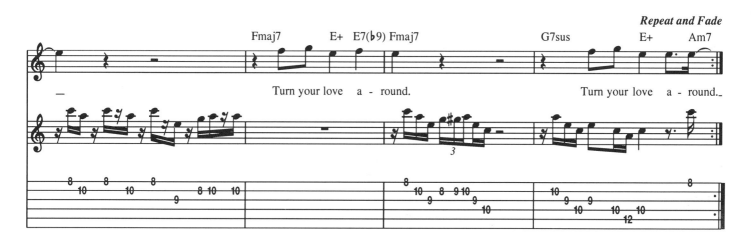

Repeat and Fade

Turn your love a-round.   Turn your love a-round.

We As Love

By Ronnie Foster

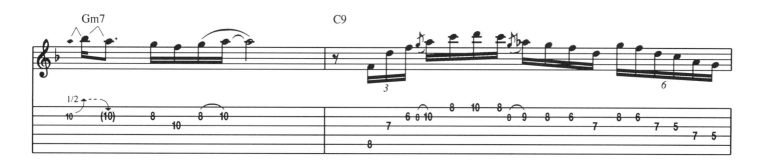

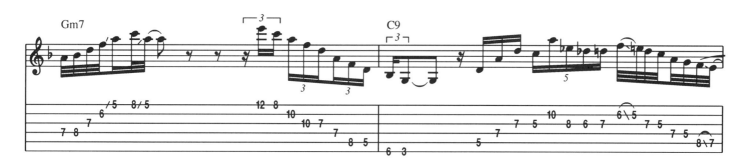

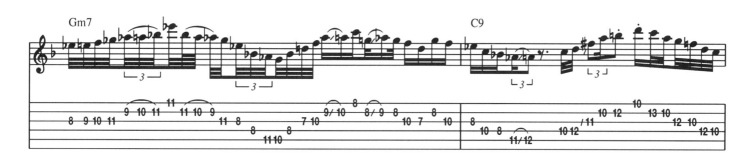

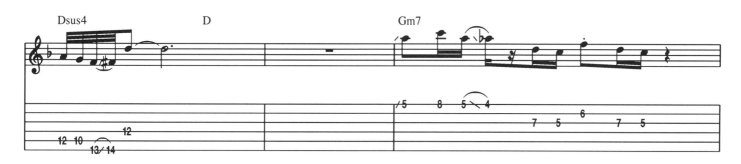

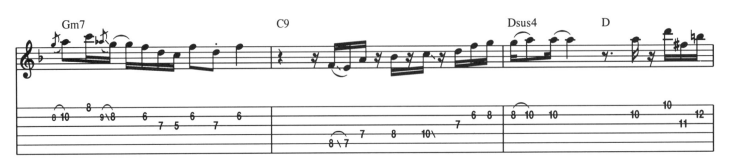

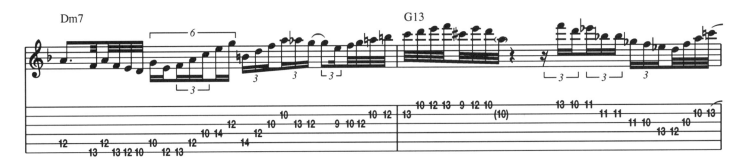

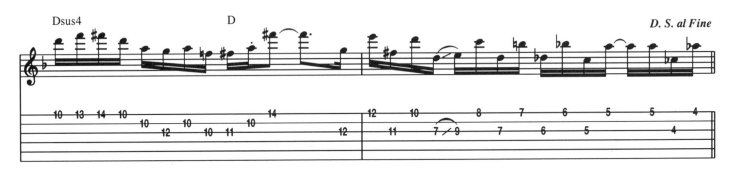

We've Got The Love

Words and Music by George Benson

Intro

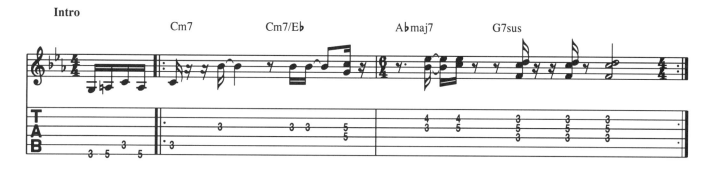

Verse

You know it hurts me when I can't be next to you, and tho' we're young, I know you

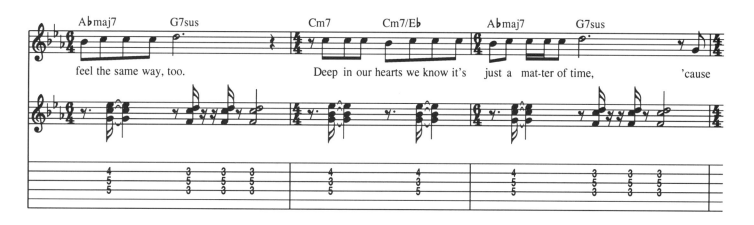

feel the same way, too. Deep in our hearts we know it's just a mat-ter of time, 'cause

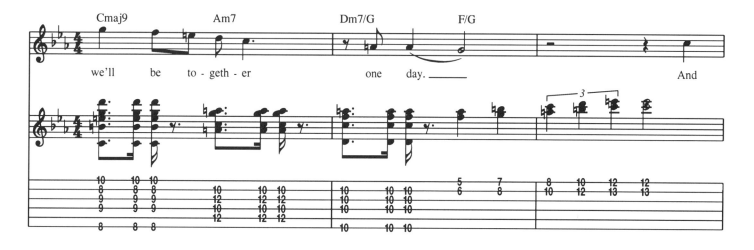

we'll be to-geth-er one day. _____ And

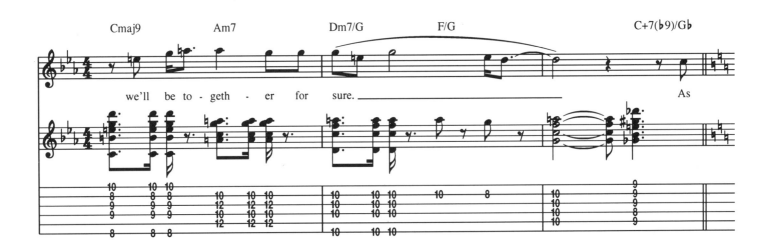

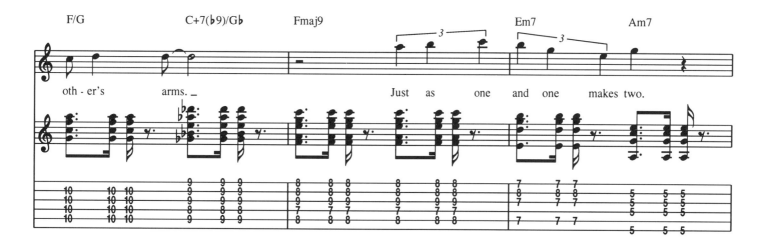

oth - er's arms. ___ Just as one and one makes two.

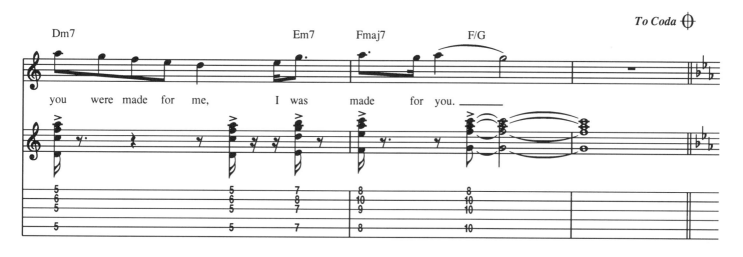

To Coda

you were made for me, I was made for you. ___

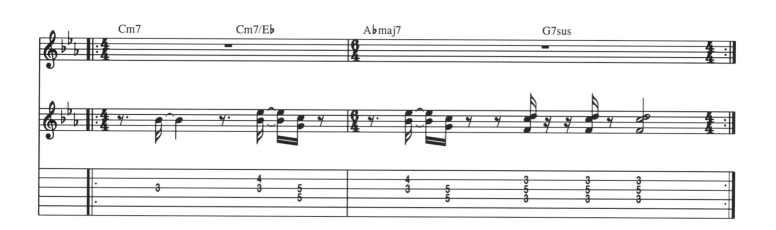

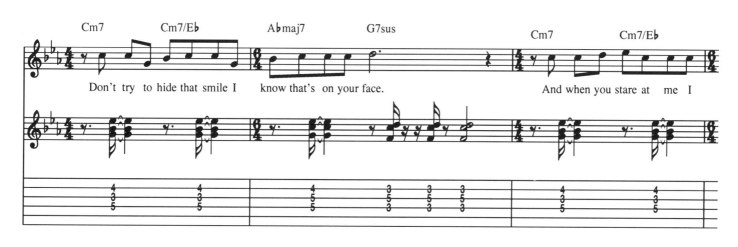

Don't try to hide that smile I know that's on your face. And when you stare at me I

look the oth-er way. And we won't give a-way what we know from the start, 'cause

D.S. al Coda

we've got the love ___ in our hearts. _____ As

⊕ *Coda*

Don't try to hide that smile I know that's on your face,

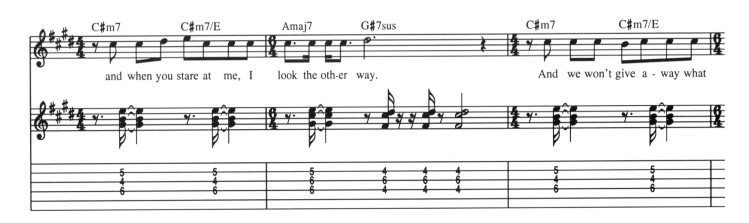

and when you stare at me, I look the oth-er way. And we won't give a-way what

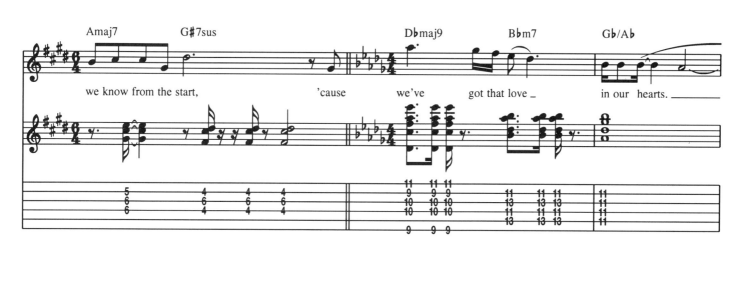

Weekend In L. A.

By George Benson

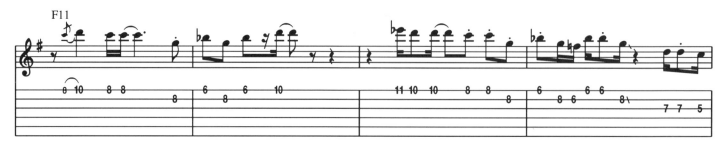

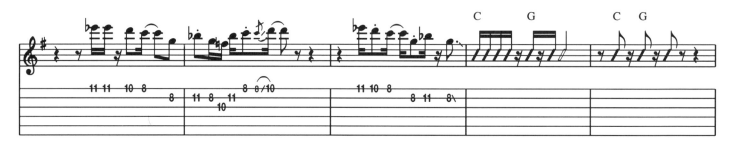

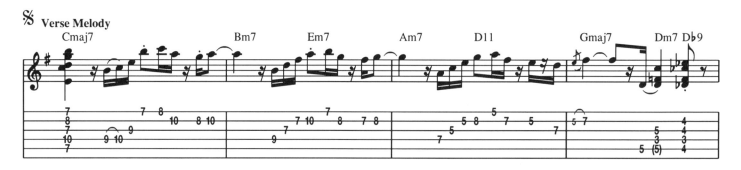

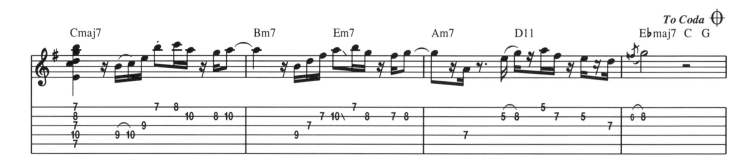

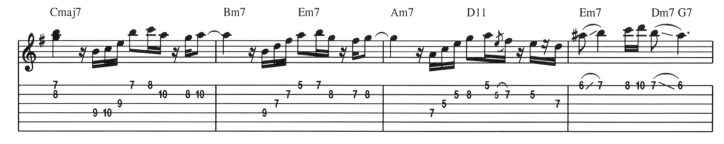

Welcome Into My World

Words and Music by George Benson

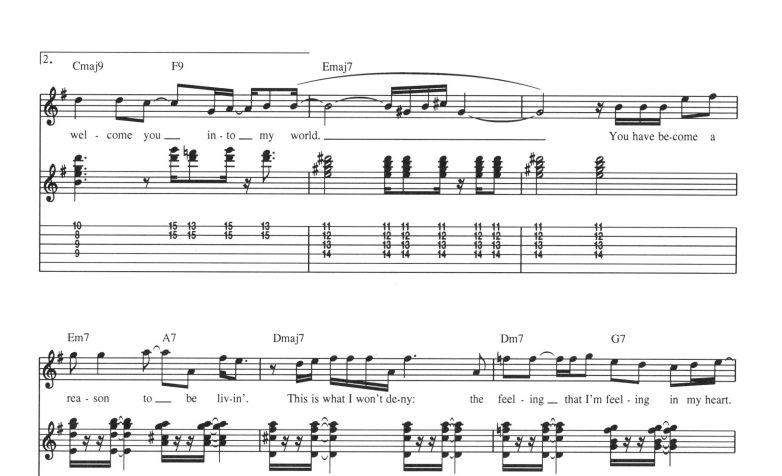

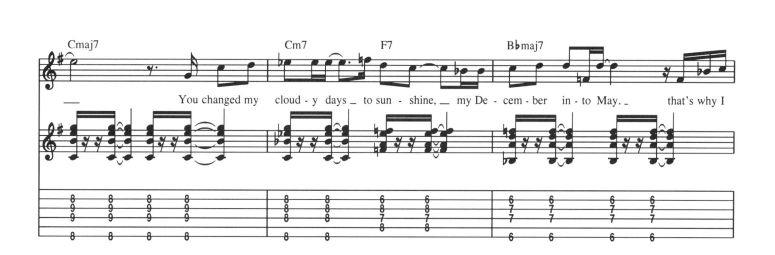

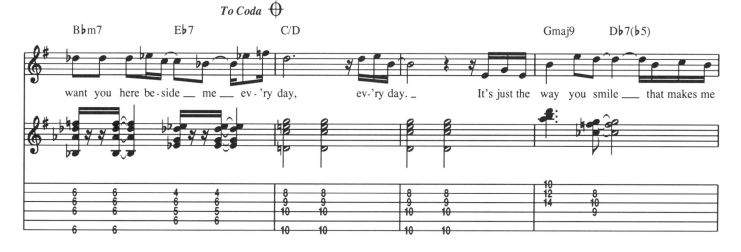

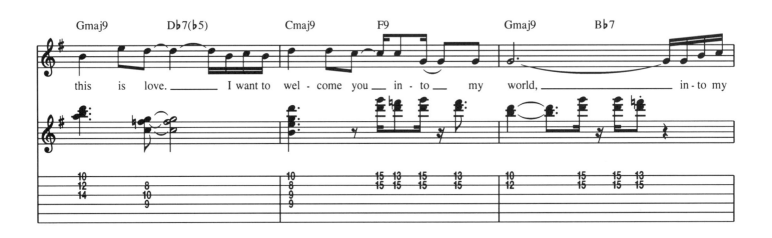

D. S. al Coda

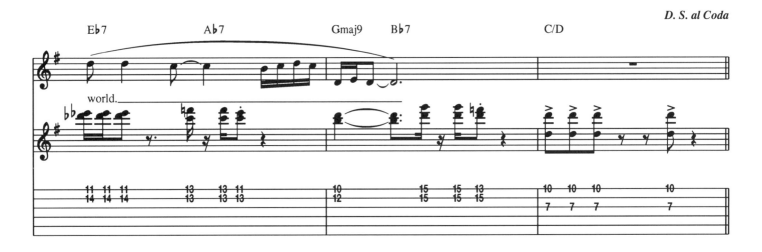

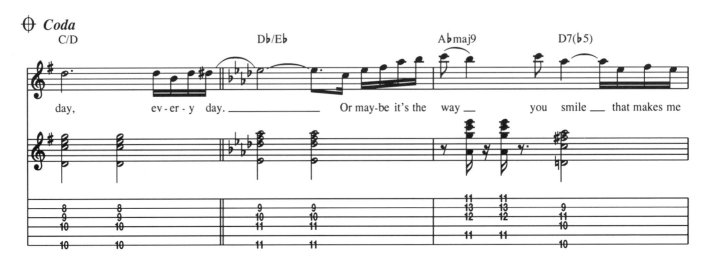

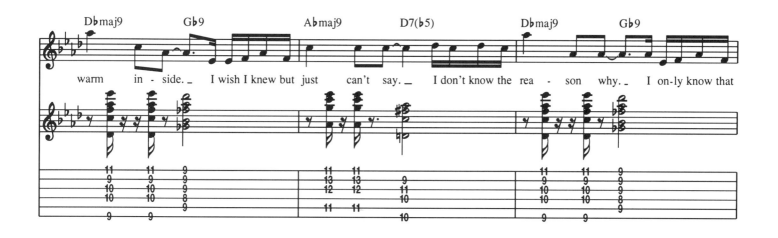

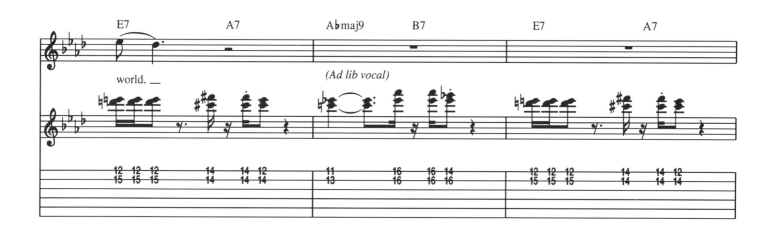

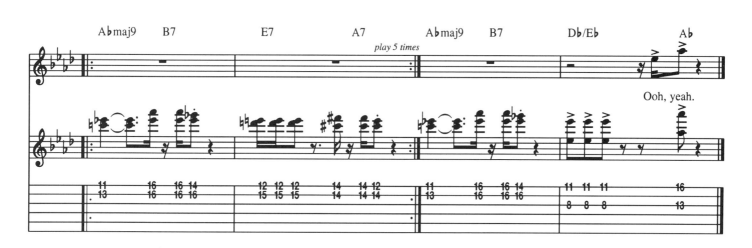

NOTATION LEGEND

RECORDED VERSIONS

THE BEST NOTE-FOR-NOTE TRANSCRIPTIONS AVAILABLE !

All Guitar and Bass Books Include Tablature

RECORDED VERSIONS FOR GUITAR

00692015	Aerosmith's Greatest Hits	$18.95
00660133	Aerosmith – Pump	$18.95
00660225	Alice In Chains – Facelift	$18.95
00694826	Anthrax – Attack Of The Killer B's	$18.95
00660227	Anthrax – Persistence Of Time	$18.95
00694797	Armored Saint – Symbol Of Salvation	$18.95
00660051	Badlands	$18.95
00694863	Beatles – Sgt. Pepper's Lonely Hearts Club Band	$18.95
00694832	Beatles – Acoustic Guitar Book	$16.95
00660140	The Beatles Guitar Book	$18.95
00699041	The Best of George Benson	$18.95
00692385	Chuck Berry	$18.95
00692200	Black Sabbath – We Sold Our Soul For Rock 'N' Roll	$18.95
00694770	Jon Bon Jovi – Blaze Of Glory	$18.95
00694774	Bon Jovi – New Jersey	$18.95
00694775	Bon Jovi – Slippery When Wet	$18.95
00694762	Cinderella – Heartbreak Station	$18.95
00692376	Cinderella – Long Cold Winter	$18.95
00692375	Cinderella – Night Songs	$18.95
00694869	Eric Clapton – Unplugged	$18.95
00692392	Eric Clapton – Crossroads Vol. 1	$22.95
00692393	Eric Clapton – Crossroads Vol. 2	$22.95
00692394	Eric Clapton – Crossroads Vol. 3	$22.95
00660139	Eric Clapton – Journeyman	$18.95
00692391	The Best of Eric Clapton	$18.95
00694873	Eric Clapton – Time Pieces	$24.95
00694788	Classic Rock	$17.95
00694793	Classic Rock Instrumentals	$16.95
00694862	Contemporary Country Guitar	$17.95
00660127	Alice Cooper – Trash	$18.95
00694840	Cream – Disraeli Gears	$14.95
00694844	Def Leppard – Adrenalize	$18.95
00692440	Def Leppard – High 'N' Dry/Pyromania	$18.95
00692430	Def Leppard – Hysteria	$18.95
00660186	Alex De Grassi Guitar Collection	$16.95
00694831	Derek And The Dominos – Layla & Other Assorted Love Songs	$19.95
00692240	Bo Diddley Guitar Solos	$18.95
00660175	Dio – Lock Up The Wolves	$18.95
00660178	Willie Dixon	$24.95
00694800	FireHouse	$18.95
00660184	Lita Ford – Stiletto	$18.95
00694807	Danny Gatton – 88 Elmira St	$17.95
00694848	Genuine Rockabilly Guitar Hits	$19.95
00694798	George Harrison Anthology	$19.95
00660326	Guitar Heroes	$17.95
00694780	Guitar School Classics	$17.95
00694768	Guitar School Greatest Hits	$17.95
00660325	The Harder Edge	$17.95
00692930	Jimi Hendrix–Are You Experienced?	$19.95
00692931	Jimi Hendrix–Axis: Bold As Love	$19.95
00660192	The Jimi Hendrix Concerts	$24.95
00692932	Jimi Hendrix–Electric Ladyland	$24.95
00660099	Jimi Hendrix–Radio One	$24.95
00660024	Jimi Hendrix–Variations On A Theme: Red House	$18.95
00660029	Buddy Holly	$18.95
00660200	John Lee Hooker – The Healer	$18.95
00660169	John Lee Hooker – A Blues Legend	$17.95
00694850	Iron Maiden – Fear Of The Dark	$19.95
00694761	Iron Maiden – No Prayer For The Dying	$18.95
00693097	Iron Maiden – Seventh Son Of A Seventh Son	$18.95
00693096	Iron Maiden – Power Slave/Somewhere In Time	$19.95
00693095	Iron Maiden	$22.95
00694833	Billy Joel For Guitar	$18.95
00660147	Eric Johnson Guitar Transcriptions	$18.95
00694799	Robert Johnson – At The Crossroads	$19.95

00660226	Judas Priest – Painkiller	$18.95
00693185	Judas Priest – Vintage Hits	$18.95
00693186	Judas Priest – Metal Cuts	$18.95
00693187	Judas Priest – Ram It Down	$18.95
00694764	Kentucky Headhunters – Pickin' On Nashville	$18.95
00694795	Kentucky Headhunters – Electric Barnyard	$18.95
00660050	B. B. King	$18.95
00660068	Kix – Blow My Fuse	$18.95
00694806	L.A. Guns – Hollywood Vampires	$18.95
00694794	Best Of Los Lobos	$18.95
00660199	The Lynch Mob – Wicked Sensation	$18.95
00693412	Lynyrd Skynyrd	$18.95
00660174	Yngwie Malmsteen – Eclipse	$18.95
00694845	Yngwie Malmsteen – Fire And Ice	$18.95
00694756	Yngwie Malmsteen – Marching Out	$18.95
00694755	Yngwie Malmsteen's Rising Force	$18.95
00660001	Yngwie Malmsteen Rising Force – Odyssey	$18.95
00694757	Yngwie Malmsteen – Trilogy	$18.95
00692880	Metal Madness	$17.95
00694792	Metal Church – The Human Factor	$18.95
00660229	Monster Metal Ballads	$19.95
00694802	Gary Moore – Still Got The Blues	$18.95
00694872	Vinnie Moore – Meltdown	$18.95
00693495	Vinnie Moore – Time Odyssey	$18.95
00694830	Ozzy Osbourne – No More Tears	$18.95
00694855	Pearl Jam – Ten	$18.95
00693800	Pink Floyd – Early Classics	$18.95
00660188	Poison – Flesh & Blood	$18.95
00693866	Poison – Open Up & Say…AHH	$18.95
00693865	Poison – Look What The Cat Dragged In	$18.95
00693864	The Best Of Police	$18.95
00692535	Elvis Presley	$18.95
00693910	Ratt – Invasion of Your Privacy	$18.95
00693911	Ratt – Out Of The Cellar	$18.95
00660060	Robbie Robertson	$18.95
00694760	Rock Classics	$17.95
00693474	Rock Superstars	$17.95
00694836	Richie Sambora – Stranger In This Town	$18.95
00694805	Scorpions – Crazy World	$18.95
00694796	Steelheart	$18.95
00694180	Stryper – In God We Trust	$18.95
00694824	Best Of James Taylor	$14.95
00694846	Testament – The Ritual	$18.95
00660084	Testament – Practice What You Preach	$18.95
00694765	Testament – Souls Of Black	$18.95
00694767	Trixter	$18.95
00694410	The Best of U2	$18.95
00694411	U2 – The Joshua Tree	$18.95
00660137	Steve Vai – Passion & Warfare	$24.95
00660136	Stevie Ray Vaughan – In Step	$18.95
00660058	Stevie Ray Vaughan – Lightnin' Blues 1983 – 1987	$22.95
00694835	Stevie Ray Vaughan – The Sky Is Crying	$18.95
00694776	Vaughan Brothers – Family Style	$18.95
00660196	Vixen – Rev It Up	$18.95
00660054	W.A.S.P. – The Headless Children	$18.95
00694787	Warrant – Dirty Rotten Filthy Stinking Rich	$18.95
00694781	Warrant – Cherry Pie	$18.95
00694786	Winger	$18.95
00694782	Winger – In The Heart Of The Young	$18.95

Prices and availability subject to change without notice.

For more information, see your local music dealer, or write to:

Hal Leonard Publishing Corporation

P.O. Box 13819 Milwaukee, Wisconsin 53213

EASY RECORDED VERSIONS FOR GUITAR

00660159	The Best Of Aerosmith	$14.95
00660134	Aerosmith – Pump	$14.95
00694785	Beatles Best	$14.95
00660117	Black Sabbath – We Sold Our Soul For Rock 'N' Roll	$12.95
00660094	The Best of Eric Clapton	$14.95
00699331	Early Rock Hits	$12.95
00660097	Jimi Hendrix – Are You Experienced?	$12.95
00660195	Jimi Hendrix – Axis: Bold As Love	$12.95
00660201	Jimi Hendrix – Electric Ladyland	$12.95
00660122	Lynyrd Skynyrd	$14.95
00660173	Pink Floyd- Dark Side of the Moon	$14.95
00660118	Pink Floyd – Early Classics	$12.95
00660206	The Best Of The Police	$14.95
00699332	Rock And Roll Classics	$12.95
00660107	Rock Superstars	$12.95
00660096	The Best of U2	$14.95
00694839	Unplugged – Acoustic Rock Guitar Hits	$12.95
00694784	Vaughan Brothers – Family Style	$14.95

BASS RECORDED VERSIONS

00660135	Aerosmith – Pump	$14.95
00660103	Beatles Bass Book	$14.95
00694803	Best Bass Rock Hits	$12.95
00660116	Black Sabbath – We Sold Our Soul For Rock 'N' Roll	$14.95
00694771	Jon Bon Jovi – Blaze Of Glory	$12.95
00694773	Bon Jovi – New Jersey	$14.95
00694772	Bon Jovi – Slippery When Wet	$12.95
00660187	The Best Of Eric Clapton	$14.95
00692878	Heavy Metal Bass Licks	$14.95
00660132	The Buddy Holly Bass Book	$12.95
00660130	Iron Maiden – Powerslave/Somewhere In Time	$17.95
00660106	Judas Priest – Metal Cuts	$17.95
00694758	Lynch Mob – Wicked Sensation	$16.95
00660121	Lynyrd Skynyrd Bass Book	$14.95
00660082	Yngwie Malmsteen's Rising Force	$9.95
00660119	Pink Floyd – Early Classics	$14.95
00660172	Pink Floyd – Dark Side Of The Moon	$14.95
00660207	The Best of the Police	$14.95
00660085	Rockabilly Bass Book	$14.95
00694783	Best Of U2	$18.95
00694777	Stevie Ray Vaughan – In Step	$14.95
00694778	Stevie Ray Vaughan – Lightnin' Blues 1983 – 1987	$19.95
00694779	Vaughan Brothers – Family Style	$16.95
00694763	Warrant – Dirty Rotten Filthy Stinking Rich/ Cherry Pie	$16.95
00694766	Winger – Winger/In The Heart Of The Young	$16.95

DRUM RECORDED VERSIONS

00694790	Best Of Bon Jovi	$12.95
00660181	Bonham – Disregard Of Timekeeping	$14.95
06621752	Classic Rock	$12.95
00694820	Best Of Lynyrd Skynyrd	$14.95
06621751	Power Rock	$12.95
06621749	Winger – Winger/In The Heart Of The Young	$14.95

KEYBOARD RECORDED VERSIONS

00694827	Beatles Keyboard Book	$17.95
00694828	Billy Joel Keyboard Book	$17.95
00694829	Elton John Keyboard Book	$19.95